Herb Gardening
for
Canada

Laura Peters

LONE PINE

Lone Pine Publishing

© 2008 by Lone Pine Publishing
First printed in 2008   10 9 8 7 6 5 4 3 2 1
Printed in China

The Publisher: Lone Pine Publishing
10145–81 Avenue, Edmonton, AB, T6E 1W9, Canada
Website: www.lonepinepublishing.com

Library and Archives Canada Cataloguing in Publication

Peters, Laura, 1968–
      Herb gardening for Canada / Laura Peters.

Includes index.
ISBN 978-1-55105-590-9

      1. Herb gardening--Canada. 2. Herbs. I. Title.

SB351.H5P48 2008   635'.70971   C2007-906513-9

Editorial Director: Nancy Foulds
Project Editor: Sandra Bit
Editorial & Photo Coordinator: Carol Woo
Craft & Food Styling: Laura Peters
Production Manager: Gene Longson
Book Design, Layout & Production: Heather Markham
Map Design: Mike Cooke
Cover Design: Gerry Dotto
Photography: All studio photographs by Nanette Samol; outdoor photographs by Laura Peters, except as noted on page 248.

The frost free map that appears on page 6 and hardiness zones map on page 10 were adapted from a similar map from the Atlas of Canada http://atlas.gc.ca/©2007. Produced under licence from Her Majesty the Queen in Right of Canada, with permission of Natural Resources Canada.

No plant or plant extract should be consumed unless you are certain of its identity and toxicity and of your own potential for allergic reactions. This book is not a "how-to" guide for self-medicating with herbs, and herbs should always be used with caution and the advice of trained experts.

We acknowledge the financial support of the Government of Canada through the Book Publishing Industry Development Program (BPIDP) for our publishing activities.

PC: P15

Table of Contents

Introduction

What is a Herb?

This book is about herbs that have culinary, cosmetic and craft uses. You might recognize some of these uses, while others may be new to you. If you share my curiosity about plants in general, I'm confident that you'll find the 60 or so species of herbs featured here interesting enough to experiment with, regardless of your cooking or crafting expertise.

Thousands of plants have medicinal properties that have been integral to human survival since time immorial, and their medicinal value is well established. These plants are in a wide range of pharmaceuticals, some of which are life-saving drugs. The health claims for other herbs, however, are unproven and based solely on theory or tradition. Treat all medicinal herbs with respect and caution at all times. This book mentions medicinal uses of many herbs, but they are not a recommended use and are included purely for interest, particularly when herbs might be taken internally. Always consult a medical professional before using any for medicinal purposes.

That said, it is fascinating that once upon a time, people discovered that certain plants would treat particular ailments. How did they figure this out? How many people lost their lives trying to find out whether their theories were correct? It is a sobering thought.

Types of Herbs

I hope to share the joys of herbs, their smells, tastes and everything they have to offer to the artist, crafter, cook and dreamer. Grow herbs for their beauty or for their practical uses—either way, you'll continue to learn the basics of growing herbs, using their unique attributes and enjoying everything that they have to offer.

Herbs come in all forms and some cross over from one category to the next.

Roses are an example of a woody perennial, also grown as an everlasting; rose potpourri (above).

Perennials

Perennials are plants that take three or more years to complete their life cycles. This broad definition includes trees and shrubs, but more narrowly we refer to herbaceous perennials as perennials. Herbaceous perennials generally die back to the ground in autumn and start fresh with new shoots each spring. Some plants grouped with perennials do not die back completely, and others remain green all winter. Subshrubs such as thyme, and evergreen perennials such as honeysuckle or lavender, are examples of other plants grouped with perennials. Winter garden conditions vary widely across Canada; nevertheless, some perennials will flourish and provide you with an almost limitless selection of colours, sizes and forms.

Annuals

True annuals are plants that germinate, mature, bloom, set seed and die in one growing season. The plants we treat as annuals, or bedding plants, may be annuals, biennials or tender perennials. We plant them in the spring or summer and expect to enjoy them for just that year. Many biennials, if started early enough, will flower the year you plant them, and many plants that are perennial in warmer climates will grow and flower before they succumb to our cold winter temperatures.

Annuals are grouped into three categories based on how they tolerate cold weather: hardy, half-hardy or tender. Hardy annuals tolerate low temperatures and even frost. Half-hardy annuals tolerate a light frost but will be killed by a heavy one. These annuals, generally started early from seed indoors, can be planted out around the last-frost date. Tender annuals have no frost tolerance and suffer if the temperature drops to a few degrees above freezing. The advantage to these annuals is that they often withstand hot summer temperatures.

When planting annuals, consider their ability to tolerate an unexpected frost. The dates for last frost and first frost vary greatly across Canada. The map (above) shows general frost-free periods across Canada, but they can vary from year to year and within the general regions. Ask at your local garden center about frost expectations for your area. Protecting plants from frost is relatively simple—just cover them overnight with sheets, towels, burlap or even cardboard boxes. Don't use plastic because it doesn't retain heat or provide plants with any insulation.

Trees and Shrubs

Trees and shrubs are woody perennials that live for three or more years and

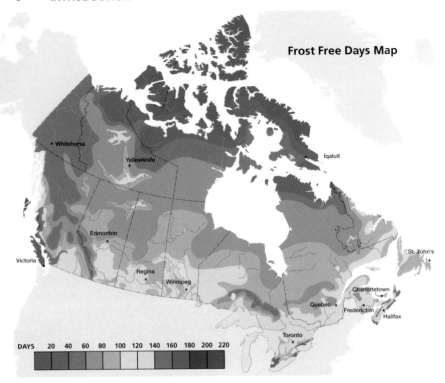

Frost Free Days Map

DAYS   20   40   60   80   100   120   140   160   180   200   220

maintain a permanent live structure above ground all year. In cold climates, a few shrubs die back to the ground each winter. The root system, protected by soil over winter, sends up new shoots in spring, and if the shrub forms flowers on new wood it will bloom that same year. Such shrubs act like herbaceous perennials, but because they are woody in their native climates they are treated as shrubs.

A tree is generally defined as a woody plant that has a single trunk and grows greater than 15' (4.6 m) tall, and a shrub is multi-stemmed and no taller than 15' (4.6 m). To complicate matters, one species may grow as a tree in favourable conditions and as a shrub in harsher sites.

Woody plants are characterized by leaf type. Deciduous plants lose all their leaves each fall or winter. Evergreen trees and shrubs do not lose their leaves in the winter and can also be needled or broad-leaved. Some plants are semi-evergreen; they are generally evergreens that in cold climates lose some or all of their leaves.

Vines and Other Herbs

Vines can be annual, perennial, tropical and woody. Vegetables produce edible seeds, roots, stems, leaves, bulbs, tubers or non-sweet fruits. Aquatic or water plants grow either in water or wet soil. Bulbs are herbs with a bulb-like base that is either at soil level or under the soil. Everlastings are grown for the purpose of drying and preserving in their natural state.

Other types of herbs include tropical plants— native to the tropics and often grown as houseplants in our colder climates.

Herb Garden Design

Herb gardens were once created according to very particular formal designs, but today they are based on individual interpretations and desires. Herbs can be integrated into any garden setting, or they can be grown together in an area of their own. Herbs can be planted in a vegetable garden for aesthetic purposes, to use space more efficiently or as companion plants for the benefits they provide.

Herbs can be planted in theme gardens or containers. An Italian garden, with tomatoes, peppers, garlic, oregano and basil, includes all of the ingredients necessary to enjoy a traditional Italian meal. In themed gardens, ease of harvesting is as important as the plants—it's just easier to have all of the plants together within reach.

Herbs can be blended into existing garden spaces, including mixed beds and borders made up of shrubs, perennials, annuals and more. Treat the herbs just as they would be normally, based on their preference for light, soil and space, depending on what type of plants they are. What you plan to do with the plant once it's established is also important.

Factors to Consider

Once you know which herbs to grow, ask yourself a few questions to help you decide where to plant and how many to plant. Will you require a lot of the herb? Will you need to grow several plants or only one? Is it a plant that you'd prefer to bring in for the winter for year-round use, or is your season long enough for it to produce the seed or fruit necessary for its use? Garlic for example, is only useful when planted in groups—having one bulb isn't very helpful. You may only want one tarragon plant, because it is perennial, grows vigorously and to a

Rosemary in a standard form (above), lavender topiary (below)

large size, but you may want half a dozen different basil plants.

Growing Herbs Indoors

An indoor herb garden has much to offer cooks, crafters and artists—you can harvest plants easily and not have to deal with the weather. Space and light are the only two components to consider when gardening indoors. Herbs can also be grown indoors alone as specimens, or feature plants. Herbs grown indoors tend to remain smaller than those grown outdoors or in their native habitats.

The biggest challenge to growing herbs indoors is lack of sufficient light. Herbs require at least five hours of direct sunlight. West- or south-facing windows are best, depending on light conditions. Keep the windows clean so that the light isn't diffused, place the plants as close to the windows as possible and rotate the containers weekly to give all sides of the plant maximum exposure to the light.

Remember as you pot herbs in containers to add organic matter, including compost, glacial dust, earthworm castings or bat guano, to ensure that they have nutrients to draw from while indoors. Fertilizing isn't necessary because the plants are simply maintaining themselves. If nutrient deficiencies begin to show, fertilize with dilute compost tea or a naturally derived or organic fertilizer once a month. If the plants become stretched or their colour fades, relocate them to a brighter spot. Harvesting regularly or pinching new growth back will also help maintain a dense habit and keep plants tidier.

Herbs grown in containers can either be grown indoors all year long, or they can brought outdoors when the risk of frost has passed. For example, woody herbs such as rosemary or kaffir lime will appreciate growing in a container in a sunny room throughout the winter, and then being moved outdoors for the summer. The additional sunlight results in flowers, fruit and new, lush growth.

Growing Herbs Outdoors

Growing herbs outdoors is as easy as it gets. Once you've chosen the right location, there's little to do other than basic care and maintenance and, of course, the harvest. You can grow your herbs on a balcony or patio, close to the kitchen, craft room or studio, or in your raised vegetable beds. Either way, herbs require the same basic care as any other plant in your garden.

Ornamental Versus Practical

The main difference between a herb garden that has been planted strictly for ornamental purposes and one that has been planted for harvesting is ease of access. If aesthetics is your only goal, then you won't need to get at your herbs very often, except for deadheading as necessary. If you plant herbs to use for practical purposes such as cooking, however, you need easy access to them to dig them up, pick the flowers or pinch back the leaves. If you always have to struggle to get to your herbs, you'll get frustrated and won't bother using them.

Garden beds planted for harvesting should be about 1 m (3 ft) wide, to allow you to reach into the bed comfortably. If you want garden beds wider than that, create several beds with paths in between them. When planting herbs specifically for cooking, put them close to your kitchen so you can harvest

Most herbs can be planted in either a garden (above) or in pots (below)

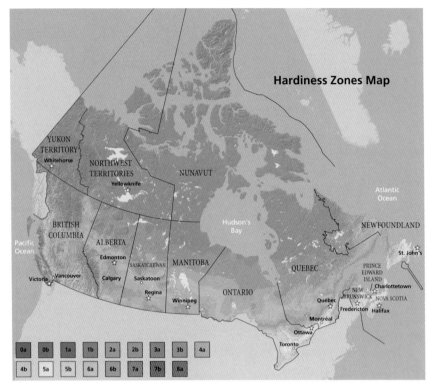

Hardiness Zones Map

YUKON TERRITORY
Whitehorse
NORTHWEST TERRITORIES
Yellowknife
NUNAVUT
Atlantic Ocean
BRITISH COLUMBIA
ALBERTA
Edmonton
SASKATCHEWAN
MANITOBA
Hudson's Bay
NEWFOUNDLAND
Pacific Ocean
St. John's
Victoria Vancouver
Calgary
Saskatoon
Regina
Winnipeg
ONTARIO
QUEBEC
PRINCE EDWARD ISLAND
Charlottetown
NEW BRUNSWICK
NOVA SCOTIA
Québec
Fredericton
Halifax
Montréal
Ottawa
Toronto

| 0a | 0b | 1a | 1b | 2a | 2b | 3a | 3b | 4a |
| 4b | 5a | 5b | 6a | 6b | 7a | 7b | 8a |

Lemon balm in a raised bed

fresh herbs conveniently, even while making a meal. Raised beds are even better, particularly if you have disabilities or are elderly, because you won't have to bend over or down to weed the beds, and you be able to reach into the bed from a sitting position if your bed has a ledge.

Hardiness Zones and Microclimates

Hardiness zones are a guideline for you to follow not only when choosing, but also when deciding where to plant, your herbs. The zones are based on the average climate conditions of each area and what plants will most likely survive there. If you're unsure of your plant hardiness zone, ask the staff at your local garden centre or a gardening savvy friend. Knowing your zone may mean the difference between planting something that will survive the winter outdoors and something that won't.

The microclimate of your own garden is influenced by such conditions as the nearness of buildings, how quickly the soil drains and whether your garden is in a low, cold hollow or on top of a windswept knoll or hillside.

The Basics

With good planning and preparation, you can enjoy a low-maintenance garden. It's a good idea to choose plants that perform well with little maintenance and that are generally pest and disease free.

Low-maintenance Herbs
Arugula
Bergamot
Borage
Catnip
Calendula
Orgegano/Marjoram
Mint
Parsley
Perilla
Safflower
Scented Geranium
Thyme

Once you know what herbs you'd like to grow in your garden, learn how best to grow them to prevent costly mistakes—plan ahead rather than correct later. Make a sketch of your garden on graph paper and include its various growing conditions to help you recognize which plants will do best where.

Plants grown in ideal conditions, or conditions close to ideal, are healthier and less prone to pests and diseases than plants growing in stressful conditions. Some plants considered high maintenance become low maintenance when grown in the right conditions. Do not try to make your garden match the growing conditions of the plants you like. Instead, choose plants to match your garden conditions.

Sun or Shade

Buildings, trees, fences and time of day all influence the amount of light that reaches your garden. There are four

Safflower (above), borage (below)

basic categories of light in the garden: full sun, partial shade, light shade and full shade. Knowing what light is available in your garden helps you decide where to put each plant.

Full sun locations, e.g., along a south-facing wall, receive direct sunlight all or most of the day. **Partial shade** or partial sun locations, e.g., along an east- or west-facing wall, receive direct sun for part of the day and shade for the rest.

Calendula (left), bergamot (right), lemon balm (below)

Light shade locations receive shade most or all of the day, but some sun gets through to ground level; e.g., small dapples of sun are visible on the ground under a small-leaved tree. **Full shade** locations, e.g., the north side of a house, receive no direct sunlight.

Remember that the intensity of the full sun varies. Heat can become trapped and magnified between city buildings, baking all but the most heat-tolerant of plants in a concrete oven. Consider how long your garden is exposed to the sun. A fully exposed area can receive up to 16 hours of sunlight a day. Even a shaded northern exposure can receive a touch of sunlight in early morning and late evening. Plants that normally wouldn't burn or scalding can be affected. Some perennials cannot fully tolerate our open blue prairie skies, so provide a suitable location for touchy plant material.

Herbs for Full Sun
Basil
Bay Laurel
Borage

Calendula
Caraway
Dill
Fenugreek
Rose
Sage
Thyme

Herbs for Full to Partial Shade
Bergamot
Lemon Balm
Lovage
Mint
Orach
Parsley
Perilla
Rosemary

Organic amendments (left to right): moisture-holding granules, earthworm castings, glacial dust, mycorrhizae, bat guano, compost, bone meal and coir fibre

Soil

Soil is the backbone of your garden, so invest in the best soil available and your plants will be amply rewarded.

Soil is made up of particles of different sizes. Sand particles are the largest. Water drains quickly out of sandy soil and nutrients are quickly washed away. Sand has lots of air and doesn't compact easily. Clay particles are the smallest and can only be seen through a microscope. Water penetrates clay very slowly and drains very slowly. Clay holds the most nutrients, but there is very little room for air, and clay compacts quite easily. Most soil is made up of a combination of different particle sizes. These soils are called loams.

The pH is the scale on which the acidity or alkalinity of the soil is analyzed. Most plants prefer a soil pH between 5.5 and 7.5. Soil-testing kits are available at most garden centres if you want to test your soil. Soil acidity influences which nutrients are available for plants. Altering the pH of your soil can take many years and is not easy. If you want to grow only one or two plants that require a soil that is more, or less, acidic, put them in a container or raised bed to make soil pH easier to control and amend.

Another aspect to consider is how quickly the water drains out of your soil. Rocky soil on a hillside drains very quickly and should be reserved for plants that grow best in very well-drained soil. Low-lying areas tend to retain water longer, and these moist areas can be planted with herbs that require a consistent water supply. Some areas may rarely drain at all; these wet spots can be used for plants that prefer boggy conditions.

Herbs for Dry Soil
Catnip
Chives
Curry
Elderberry
Lemon Balm
Onion
Thyme

Herbs for Moist Soil
Chervil
Cress
Dill
Fennel
Fenugreek
Lemongrass
Oregano/Marjoram
Sweet Cicely

Chives (above), fenugreek (centre), chicory (below)

Herbs for Sandy Soil
Anise
Chicory

Herbs for Rich Soil
Arugula
Orach

Exposure

Finally, consider the exposure in your garden. Wind, heat, cold and rain are some of the elements your garden is exposed to, and different plants are better adapted than others to the potential damage these forces can cause. Buildings, walls, fences, hills, hedges and trees can all influence your garden's exposure.

Herbs for Exposed Locations
Calendula
Dandelion
Lavender
Lemon Balm
Lemongrass
Lovage
Marigolds
Mint
Safflower
Sage

Wind in particular can damage plants. Dehydration occurs in windy locations because the plants may not be able to draw water out of the soil fast enough to replace the water lost through the leaves. Strong winds can knock down tall, stiff-stemmed perennials, and they may need to be staked in an exposed one. Use plants that are recommended for exposed sites or temper the effect of the wind with a hedge or some trees. A solid wall creates turbulence on the leeward side, while a looser structure such as a hedge breaks up the force of the wind and protects a larger area.

Preparing the Garden

Take the time before you start planting to properly prepare your garden bed—it will save time later on. First remove all weeds— the most thorough technique is to dig the bed over and pick them all out by hand—and amend the soil with organic matter.

I strongly encourage you to garden organically, particularly in your herb garden. When using plants for cooking or in creams and lotions applied to the skin or hair, it's always best to use healthy gardening practices, whether you are putting something into the soil or applying something to the plants.

Another aspect of gardening organically is using integrated pest management (IPM) to eliminate all synthesized pesticides and herbicides from your gardening regimen. Once you learn how to eliminate these toxic chemicals from your herb garden, you can do the same in your ornamental gardens. The benefits of IPM are great, and you'll find the changes subtle and easier the more frequently you put them into practice. To poison the plants, ourselves or the soil while growing them contradicts their existence completely.

That said, let me introduce you to compost, just in case you haven't met. Studies have consistently shown the benefits of gardening organically, and for the home gardener, compost truly is black gold.

Compost

Compost is known as black gold for a reason, because organic matter benefits all kinds of soils. You can compost in a pile, wooden box or purchased composter, and the process is not complicated. A pile of kitchen scraps, grass clippings and autumn leaves will eventually break down if just left alone. Use layers of dry and fresh materials, with a higher proportion of dry matter than fresh green matter. Dry matter may be chopped straw, shredded leaves and sawdust, and green matter includes vegetable scraps and grass clippings. The smaller the pieces, the faster they will break down.

Egg shells, coffee grinds and filters, tea bags, fish bones, shrimp shells and lint from your vacuum cleaner and dryer are all beneficial additions. Do not put diseased, pest-ridden material into your compost pile—you don't want to spread problems throughout your garden. Do not add dog or cat feces, used kitty litter, fats, dairy or meat; they will attract pests and smell, resulting in a mess. Remember the basics and you'll end up with black gold.

Layer in soil or finished compost to introduce the organisms that are necessary to break down the compost pile properly. Fertilizers available at garden centres speed up the composting process. Add some water if the pile seems very dry; it needs to be moist but not soggy.

Turn the pile over or poke holes in it with a pitchfork or broom handle every week or two. Air must get into the pile to speed up decomposition.

Your compost has reached the end of its cycle when you can no longer recognize the matter that went into it and the temperature no longer rises when you turn the pile. It may take as little as a month to be ready to spread onto your garden.

A byproduct of compost is compost tea, a highly concentrated mix of organisms beneficial to the soil and ultimately to your plants. Take a piece of untreated jute or muslin, or even an old cotton pillowcase, and fill it with compost. Cinch it at the top and tie it to a wooden dowel strong enough to support it when wet. Drop the "tea bag" into a rain barrel filled with water and let it steep for a few days. Dilute this compost tea to about half, and water your plants with it. I even like to use it on my indoor plants in winter. There is no better or safer fertilizer in the world, bar none.

Planting Herbs

Plant Selection

You can buy plants or start them from seed. Purchased plants may begin flowering the same year they are planted, but plants started from seed may take several years to mature. Starting plants from seed is more economical if you want many plants.

Plants and seeds are available from garden centres, the Internet, mail-order catalogues and friends and neighbours. Garden clubs or societies sometimes promote the exchange of traditional and unusual seeds and plants, and many public gardens sell seeds of rare plants. Regardless of where you find them, make sure the source is reliable and that the herbs are not diseased or pest-ridden.

Purchased herbs are sold in pots or bare-root, usually packed in moist peat moss or sawdust. Potted plants have probably been raised in the pot. Bare-root plants are typically dormant, although some of the previous year's growth may be evident or there may be new growth starting—sometimes the piece of root appears to have no evident growth, past or present. Both potted and bare-root forms are good buys, but you still need to ensure that you are getting a plant of the best quality.

Potted herbs come in many sizes. Plants in larger containers may take longer to establish and may experience more transplant shock. The advantage is that you'll likely have a mature plant in less time. Deciding what size pot to buy depends on budget and time available for the plant to reach maturity. In the long run, herbs are going to reach their mature size regardless of what size pot you buy, so choose what's best for you.

Select plants that seem to be a good size for the pot they are in. When tapped lightly out of the pot, the roots should be visible but not winding and twisting around the inside of the pot. The leaves should be a healthy colour. If they are chewed or damaged, check carefully for insects or diseases before you buy. If the plants already show these signs, do not purchase them or the problems could spread.

A trowel, soil and fertilizer are often all you need to plant herbs.

Bare-root plants are most commonly sold through mail order, but some are available in garden centres, usually in the spring. Choose roots that are dormant (without top growth). A plant already growing may take longer to establish itself— it may have too little energy to recover after growing in the stressful conditions of a plastic bag. Once you get the herbs home, plant them as soon as possible. If you have to store them briefly, water them if they are dry and keep them in a lightly shaded. Try to choose an overcast day to help avoid drying the plants, and ensure that you have enough time to complete the job. The only tool you are likely to need is a trowel.

You don't have to be conservative when arranging your herb garden— plants can be grouped casually in natural drifts. The quickest way to space out your plants is to randomly place them on the bed, mixing colours and plants as you please. Planting a small section at a time—and not allowing the roots to dry out— is especially important if you have a large bed to plant.

If you are adding just a few herbs to accent your shrub and perennial gardens, plant in random clusters of three to five herbs that will add colour, interest and impact.

Combine low-growing or spreading plants with tall or bushy ones. Keep the tallest plants towards the back of the bed and smallest plants towards the front. Leave enough room for the plants to spread—they may look lonely and far apart, but they grow quickly.

To plant potted herbs, dig a hole about the width and depth of the pot. If the beds haven't been prepared, add a trowel full of compost to the planting hole and mix it into the garden soil before adding your plant. Remove the plant from the pot. Never pull on the stem or leaves to get a plant out of a pot. It is better to cut a difficult pot off rather than risk damaging the plant. Moisten the soil to help remove the plants from their containers. Push on the bottom of the cell or pot with your thumb to ease

the plants out. If the plants were growing in an undivided tray then you will have to gently untangle the roots. If the roots are very tangled, immerse them in water and wash some of the soil away to help free the plants from one another. If you must handle the plant, hold it by a leaf to avoid crushing the stems. Remove and discard any damaged leaves or growth.

Tease a few roots out of the soil ball to get the plant growing in the right direction. If the roots have become densely wound around the inside of the pot, cut into the root mass with a sharp knife to encourage new growth.

Insert your trowel into the soil and pull it towards you, creating a wedge. Place your plant into the hole and firm the soil around the plant with your hands. It should be buried to the same level that it was at in the pot, or a little higher, to allow for the soil to settle. Fill the soil in around the roots and firm it down. Water the plant well as soon as you have planted it, and regularly until it has established itself.

If you are adding just one or two plants and do not want to prepare an entire bed, dig a hole twice as wide and deep as the root ball. Add a little peat moss for improved air circulation and water retention, and to lighten up heavy, clay-based soils. Add slow release organic amendments, such as compost or a mycorrizae-based product, to the backfill of soil that you spread around the plant.

Finally, poke the identification tags into the soil next to each plant. Next spring, the tags will help you identify each herb.

In the first month after planting, just water the herbs regularly, weed and watch for pests. It helps to spread a protective mulch around the plants. You probably won't have to fertilize in the first year. If you do want to fertilize, wait until your new plants have started healthy new growth then apply a weak organic fertilizer.

More than one herb can grow well in the same pot.

Planting Herbs into Containers

Herbs can also be grown in planters for portable displays that can be moved about the garden. Many herbs can grow in the same container without any fresh potting soil for five or six years. Be sure to fertilize and water them more often than plants in the ground. Dig your finger deep into the soil around the plant to see if it needs water. Too much water causes root rot.

Always use a good quality potting mix or a soil mix intended for containers in your planters. Don't use garden soil because it quickly loses its structure and becomes a solid lump, preventing air, water and roots from penetrating into the soil.

Containers are exposed to baking heat in summer. The soil dries out quickly in hot weather and becomes waterlogged after a couple of rainy days. Not all plants are tough enough to survive these conditions. Some invasive herbs such as mint are good choices for containers because their spread is controlled, but they are very hardy.

Herbs in planters are also more susceptible to winter damage than plants in the garden, because sides of the container are exposed to temperature fluctuations and provide very little insulation. The container itself may crack in a deep freeze. The simplest thing to do to get planters through a tough Canadian winter is to move them to a more sheltered spot. Most perennials require some cold in the winter to flower the next year, so find a spot that is still cold, but provides some shelter. An unheated garage, enclosed porch or garden shed will offer your plants more protection than they would get sitting in the great outdoors.

Basement window wells are also good places: they are sheltered, below ground and receive some heat from the window. Wait until the soil in the pots has frozen to discourage mice from making their home in the straw and feeding on the roots, and to prevent root rot. Layer straw at the bottom of the well, sit your pots on the straw, and then cover them with more straw.

The pots themselves can be weatherproofed before you put your plants into them—doing this might also be useful for high-rise dwellers with balcony gardens. Put a layer of Styrofoam™ insulation or "packing peanuts" at the bottom and around the inside of the pot before you add your soil and plants, making sure that excess water can still drain freely from the container. Commercial planter insulating materials are also available at garden centres.

Finally, you can bury planters in the garden for the winter. Find an open space, dig a hole deep enough to sink the planter up to its rim. Large planters require an extensive excavation or even the use of a backhoe to dig deeply enough to fit the entire pot. Another disadvantage is that recovering the planter in the spring can be messy.

Growing Perennials as Annuals

Many herbs grown as annuals here are actually perennials or shrubs that are native to warmer climates and unable to survive our cold winters. Some tropical perennials are given special treatment to help them survive winter, or they are simply brought inside and treated as houseplants in the colder months.

A reverse hardening-off process is used to acclimatize plants to an indoor environment. Plants such as scented geranium and heliotrope, which are grown in the sun all summer, should be gradually moved to shady garden spots. They develop more efficient leaves that are capable of surviving in the comparatively limited light indoors.

Perennial herbs with tuberous roots can be stored over winter and replanted in late winter or early spring. Dig up plants in fall after they die back but before the ground freezes. Shake the loose dirt away from the roots and let them dry out a bit in a cool, dark place. Once they are dry and clean, dust them with an anti-fungal powder (found at garden centres) and store them in moist peat moss or coarse sawdust. Keep them in a dark, dry place that is cold but doesn't freeze. Pot them if they start to sprout, and keep them in moist soil in a bright window. Pot them up by late winter or early spring whether they have already started sprouting or not, so they will be ready for spring planting.

If winter storage sounds like too much work, replace your annual herbs each year and leave the hard work to the growers.

Perennial Herbs Grown as Annuals
Curry
Oregano
Vietnamese Coriander

Curry (above), oregano (centre)

Vietnamese coriander (below)

Caring for Your Herbs

Many herbs require little care, but all will benefit from a few maintenance basics. Weeding, pruning, deadheading and staking are just a few of the chores that, when done regularly, minimize major work.

Weeding

Controlling weeds is one of the most important things to do in your garden. Weeds compete with herbs for light, nutrients and space. Weeds can also harbour pests and diseases. Try to prevent weeds from germinating. If they do, pull them out while they are still small before they have a chance to flower, set seed and start a whole new generation of problems.

Weeds can be pulled out by hand or with a hoe. Quickly scuffing across the soil surface with the hoe will pull out small weeds and sever larger ones from their roots. A layer of mulch is an excellent way to suppress weeds.

Mulching

Mulches prevent weed seeds from germinating by blocking out the light. Soil temperatures remain more consistent and more moisture is retained under a layer of mulch. Mulch also prevents soil erosion during heavy rain or strong winds. Organic mulches consist of compost, bark chips, shredded leaves or grass clippings. Organic mulches are desirable because they improve the soil and add nutrients as they break down.

In spring, spread about 5 cm (2") of mulch around your plants, keeping the area immediately around their crowns or stems clear. Mulch that is too close can trap moisture and prevent good air circulation, encouraging disease. If the layer of mulch disappears into the soil over summer, replenish it.

Put a fresh layer of mulch, up to 10 cm (4") thick, around the plants for winter protection once the ground freezes in fall. This mulch is particularly important if you can't depend on a steady layer of snow to cover your garden in the winter. You can cover the plants with dry material such as straw, pine needles, finely shredded bark fines or shredded leaves.

Keep in mind that as the ground freezes, so too may your pile of potential mulch. One solution is to cover most of the bed with mulch, leaving only the plants exposed, before the ground freezes. Put extra mulch, needed to cover the plants, in a large plastic bag or your wheelbarrow and put it somewhere that takes longer to freeze, perhaps the garage or garden shed. Once the ground is completely frozen, you use that mulch to cover the plants.

In late winter or early spring, once the weather starts to warm up, pull the mulch layer off the plants and see if they have started growing. If they have, you can pull the mulch back, but keep it nearby in case you need to put it back on to protect the tender new growth from a late frost. Once your plants are well on their way and you are no longer worried about frost, remove the protective mulch completely. Compost the old mulch and apply a new spring mulch.

Deadheading

Deadheading—the removal of flowers once they are finished blooming—keeps plants looking tidy, prevents the plant from spreading seeds (and therefore seedlings) throughout the garden, often prolongs blooming and helps prevent pest and disease problems.

Deadheading is not necessary for every plant. Some plants with seedheads are left in place to provide interest in the garden over winter. Other plants are short-lived and by leaving some of the seedheads in place you encourage future generations to replace the old plants.

Flowers can be pinched off by hand or snipped off with hand pruners. Bushy plants that have many tiny flowers, particularly ones that have a short bloom period such as thyme, can be more aggressively pruned back with garden shears once they are done flowering. Shearing some plants such as oregano will promote new growth and possibly blooms later in the season.

Herbs Grown for their Seeds
Aniseed
Arugula
Basil
Caraway
Dill
Coriander
Fennel
Lovage
Nasturtium
Perilla
Safflower

Herbs that Self-seed
Arugula
Chives
Lemon Balm
Red Valerian
Scented Geranium
Sweet Cicely

Nasturtium seeds

Red valerian

Pruning

Many plants benefit from some grooming. Resilient health, plentiful blooming and more compact growth are signs of a well-groomed garden. Pinching, thinning and disbudding plants before they flower enhances the beauty of the herb garden. The methods for pruning are simple, but some experimentation is required to get the right.

Thinning is done to clump-forming plants such as bee balm early in the year when shoots have just emerged. These plants develop a clump of stems that allows very little air or light into the centre of the plant. Removing half of the shoots when they first emerge will increase air circulation and prevent diseases such as powdery mildew. The increased light encourages more compact growth and more flowers. Throughout the growing season, thin any growth that is weak, diseased or growing in the wrong direction.

Trimming or pinching plants is a simple procedure, but timing it correctly and achieving just the right look can be tricky. Early in the year, before the flower buds have appeared, trim the plant to encourage new side shoots. Stem by stem, remove the tip and some stem of the plant just above a leaf or pair of leaves. If you have a lot of plants, you can trim off the tops with your hedge shears to one-third of the height you expect the plants to reach. The growth that begins to emerge can be pinched again. Beautiful layered effects can be achieved by staggering the trimming times by a week or two.

Give plants enough time to set buds and flower. Most spring-flowering plants cannot be pinched back or they will not flower. Early summer or mid-summer bloomers should be pinched only once, as early in the season as possible. Late summer and fall bloomers can be pinched several times but leave them alone past June. Don't pinch the plant if flower buds have formed—it may not have enough energy or time left in the year to develop a new set of buds. Experimentation and keeping detailed notes will improve your pinching skills.

Staking

A few plants will need some support to look their best. Plants that develop tall spikes require each spike to be staked individually. Push a strong, narrow pole such as a bamboo stake into the ground early in the year and tie the spike to the stake as it grows. A forked branch can also be used to support single-stem plants.

Many plants get top-heavy and tend to flop over once they reach a certain height. A wire hoop, sometimes called a peony ring, is the most unobtrusive way to hold up such a plant. When the plant is young, push the legs of the peony ring into the ground around it and as the plant grows up, the wire or plastic ring supports it. At the same time the bushy growth hides the ring. Wire tomato cages can also be used.

Support plants with floppy tangles of stems with twiggy branches inserted into the ground around them.

Some people consider any stakes to be unsightly. To reduce the need for staking, don't use a richer soil than is recommended—very rich soil causes many plants to produce weak, leggy growth prone to falling over. Also, a plant that likes full sun will be stretched out and leggy if grown in the shade. You can also mix in plants that have a more stable structure between the plants that need support. A floppy plant may still fall over slightly, but only as far as its neighbour will allow. Many plants are available in compact varieties that don't require staking.

Herbs that May Require Staking or Support
Bay Laurel
Dill
Hops
Hyssop
Licorice
Orach
Tarragon

Some herbs grow large enough to require staking.

Watering

Many plants need little supplemental watering if they have been planted in their preferred conditions and are given a moisture-retaining mulch. The rule of watering is to water thoroughly and infrequently, and make sure the water penetrates deeply into the soil.

Fertilizing

If you prepare your beds well and add new compost to them each spring, you should not need to add extra fertilizer. If you have a limited amount of compost, you can mix a slow-release organic fertilizer into the soil around your herbs in the spring. Some plants are heavy feeders that need additional supplements throughout the growing season.

Many organic fertilizers are available at garden centres. Always use the recommended quantity, because too much fertilizer will do more harm than good.

Propagation

Learning to propagate your own plants is an interesting and challenging aspect of gardening that can save you money, but it also takes time and space. Seeds, cuttings and divisions are the three methods of increasing your plant population. There are benefits and problems associated with each method.

Seeds

Starting herbs from seed is a great way to propagate many plants that grow easily from seed and flower within a year or two of being transplanted into the garden. You can buy seeds or collect them from your own or a friend's garden. Remember that some cultivars and varieties don't pass on their desirable traits to their offspring. Other plants take a very long time to germinate, if they germinate at all, and an even longer time to grow to flowering size.

A few basic rules exist for starting all seeds. Some seeds can be started directly in the garden, but it is easier to control temperature and moisture levels and to provide a sterile environment if you start the seeds indoors. Seeds can be started in pots or, if you need a lot of plants, in flats. Use a sterile soil mix intended for starting seeds. The soil will need to be kept moist but not soggy. Most seeds germinate in moderately warm temperatures of about 14–21° C (57°–70° F). Seed-starting supplies including plastic seed-tray dividers (often called plug trays) and heating coils or pads are available at garden centres.

All seedlings are susceptible to a problem called "damping off," which is caused by soil-borne fungal organisms. An afflicted seedling looks as though someone has pinched the stem at soil level, causing the plant to topple over.

Some materials for starting seeds and a prepared seed tray

The pinched area blackens and the seedling dies. Sterile soil mix, air circulation and evenly moist soil help prevent this problem. Products are also available at your local garden centre to prevent damping off.

Fill your pot or seed tray with the soil mix and firm it down slightly—not too firmly or the soil will not drain—and wet the soil. Plant only one type of seed per pot or flat. Large seeds can be placed individually and spaced out in pots or trays. If you have divided inserts for your trays you can plant one or two seeds per section. Sprinkle small seeds more randomly. Mix tiny seeds with some very fine sand and spread on the soil surface. These tiny seeds may not need to be covered with any more soil. The medium-sized seeds can be lightly covered and the larger seeds can be pressed into the soil and then lightly covered. Do not cover seeds that need to be exposed to light in order to germinate. Water the seeds using the very fine spray of a hand-held spray bottle if the soil starts to dry out.

To keep the environment moist, place pots inside clear plastic bags. Change the bag or turn it inside out when condensation starts to build up and drip. Many seed trays come with clear plastic covers, which keep the moisture in. Remove the covers once the seeds have germinated.

Seeds generally do not require a lot of light to germinate, so pots or trays can be kept in a warm, out of the way place. Once the seeds have germinated, place them in a bright location but out of direct sun. Transplant the herbs to individual pots once they have three or four true leaves. Plants in plug trays can be left until neighbouring leaves start to touch each other, then transplant them to pots.

The seed itself provides all the nutrition the seedling will need. Fertilizing causes young seedlings to produce soft, spindly growth that is susceptible to attack by insects and diseases. A fertilizer, diluted to ¼ or ½ strength, can be used once seedlings have four or five true leaves.

Many seeds will easily grow as soon as they are planted, but others need to have their defences lowered before they will germinate. Some seeds also produce poisonous chemicals in their seed coats to deter insects. Some thick-coated seeds can be soaked for a day or two in water to promote germination, thus mimicking the end of the dry season and the beginning of the rainy season, which is when the plant would germinate in its natural environment. Other thick-coated seeds need to have their seed coats scratched to allow moisture to penetrate the seed coat and prompt germination. Nick the seeds

Grow lights (above), chamomile repels insects and fungus (below)

Cinnamon powder is a natural fungicide and has been shown to be particularly effective against damping-off. In addition, weak, cooled chamomile tea is another natural fungicide.

with a knife or gently rub them between two sheets of sand paper. Leave the seeds in a dry place for a day or so before planting them to give the seeds a chance to get ready for germination before they are exposed to water.

Plants from northern climates often have seeds that wait until spring before they germinate. These seeds must be given a period of cold before they will

Herbs planted in a strawberry planter

The lid lets light in and collects some heat during the day and prevents rain from damaging tender plants. If the interior gets too hot, the lid can be raised for ventilation. A hot frame is insulated and has heating coils in the floor to prevent the soil from freezing or to maintain a constant soil temperature for germinating seeds, or rooting cuttings.

Herbs to Start from Seed
Arugula
Caraway
Chervil
Dill
Marigold
Orach
Parsley
Scented Geranium
Strawberry

germinate. You can put the seeds in a pot or tray in the refrigerator for up to two months, but check them regularly and don't allow them to dry out. A less space-consuming method is to mix the seeds with some moistened sand, peat or sphagnum moss in a sealable sandwich bag and pop it in the refrigerator for up to two months, again being sure the sand or moss doesn't dry out. The seeds can then be planted in the pot or tray.

A cold frame can protect tender plants over the winter, start vegetable seeds early in the spring, harden plants off before moving them to the garden, protect fall-germinating seedlings and young cuttings or divisions, and start seeds that need a cold treatment. This mini-greenhouse structure is built so that ground level on the inside of the cold frame is lower than on the outside. The angled, hinged lid is fitted with glass. The soil around the outside of the cold frame insulates the plants inside.

Cuttings

Cuttings are an excellent way to propagate varieties and cultivars that you really like but that don't come true from seed or that don't produce seed at all. Each cutting will grow into a reproduction of the parent plant. Cuttings are taken from the stems of some plants and the roots of others.

Stem Cuttings

Stem cuttings are generally taken in the spring and early summer. Avoid taking cuttings from plants that are in flower—plants that are busy growing are full of the right hormones to promote quick root growth, not busy reproducing. If you do take cuttings from plants that are flowering be sure to remove the flowers and the buds to divert the plant's energy back into growing.

Cuttings need to be kept in a warm, humid place to root, which makes them very prone to fungal diseases. Providing proper sanitation and encouraging quick rooting will increase the survival rate of your cuttings.

Debate exists over what the size of cuttings should be. A small cutting is 2–5 cm (1–2") long and a large cutting is 10–15 cm (4–6") long. You can try different sizes to see what works best for you. Determine the size of cuttings by the number of leaf nodes on the cutting. You will want at least three or four nodes (the node is where the leaf joins the stem, and it is from here that the new roots will grow). The base of the cutting will be just below a node. Strip the leaves gently from the first and second nodes, and plant them below the soil. The new plants will grow from the nodes above the soil. The leaves can be left in place on the cutting above ground. Sometimes there is a lot of space between nodes, so your cutting will be longer than recommended. Some plants with almost no space at all between nodes can be cut to the recommended length. Gently remove the leaves from the lower half of the cutting. Plants with several nodes close together often root quickly and abundantly.

Always use a sharp, sterile knife to make the cuttings. Cut straight across the stem. Once you have stripped the leaves, you can dip the end of the cutting into a rooting-hormone powder intended for softwood cuttings. Sprinkle the powder onto a piece of paper and dip the cuttings into it. Discard any extra powder left on the paper. Tap or blow the extra powder off the cutting. Your cuttings are now prepared for planting.

The sooner you plant your cuttings the better. Plant the cuttings the same way you would seeds, and keep in a warm place, about 18–21° C (65–70° F), in bright, indirect light.

Strawberry planted with yarrow

Most cuttings will require from one to four weeks to root. After two weeks, give the cutting a gentle tug. You will feel resistance if roots have formed. If the cutting feels as though it can pull out of the soil mix then gently push it back down and leave it for longer. New growth is also a good sign that your cutting has rooted. Some gardeners leave the cuttings alone until they can see roots through the holes in the bottoms of the pots. Uncover the cuttings once they have developed roots.

Apply a foliar feed when the cuttings show new leaf growth. Plants quickly absorb nutrients through the leaves; therefore, you can avoid stressing the

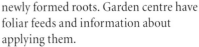

Left to right: trim the lower leaves of your cutting; cuttings with strong root growth are ready for potting; dip the end in rooting hormone; firm soil gently around cutting; several cuttings can grow in one pot until they show new growth

newly formed roots. Garden centre have foliar feeds and information about applying them.

Once your cuttings have rooted and have established themselves, they can be potted up individually. If you rooted several cuttings in one pot or tray, the roots may have tangled together. If gentle pulling doesn't separate them, take the entire clump and rinse some of the soil away. That should free the roots enough to separate the plants.

Pot the young plants in a sterile potting soil. Move them into a sheltered area of the garden or a cold frame and grow until they are large enough to plant in the garden. They may need some protection over the first winter. Keep them in the cold frame if they are still in pots. Give them an extra layer of mulch if they have been planted out.

Basal Cuttings

Basal cuttings involve removing the new growth from the main clump and rooting it in the same manner as stem cuttings. Many plants send up new shoots or plantlets around their bases. Often, the plantlets will already have a

few roots growing. The young plants develop quickly and may even grow to flowering size the first summer. You may have to cut back some of the top growth of the shoot because the tiny developing roots won't be able to support a lot of top growth. Treat these cuttings the same way as a stem cutting.

Root Cuttings

Dandelions are well known for foiling every attempt to eradicate them: even the smallest piece of root left in the ground can sprout a new plant. Other perennials share this trait, and the main difference between starting root cuttings and stem cuttings is that the root cuttings must be kept fairly dry because they can rot easily.

Take cuttings from the fleshy roots of certain plants in early- or mid-spring when the ground is just starting to warm up and the roots are just about to break dormancy. At this time, the roots of the plants are full of nutrients, which the plants stored the previous summer and fall, and hormones are initiating growth. Wet the soil around the plant so that you can loosen it enough to get to the roots.

Keep the roots slightly moist, but not wet, while you are rooting them, and keep track of which end is up. Roots must be planted in a vertical, not horizontal, position on the soil, and roots need to be kept in the orientation they held while previously attached to the parent plant. People use different methods to recognize the top from the bottom of the roots; some gardeners cut straight across the tops and diagonally across the bottoms.

You do not want very young or very old roots. Very young roots are usually white and quite soft; very old roots are tough and woody. The roots you should use will be tan coloured and still fleshy. To prepare your root, cut out the section you will be using with a sterile knife. Cut the root into pieces that are 2.5–5 cm (1–2") long. Remove any side roots before planting the sections in pots or planting trays. Use the same type of soil mix the seeds and stem cuttings were started in. Poke the pieces vertically into the soil and leave a tiny bit of the top poking up out of the soil.

Keep the pots in a warm place out of direct sunlight and don't over-water. The plants will send up new shoots once they have rooted. They can be planted in the same manner as stem cuttings (see p. 28).

Rhizomes are the easiest root cuttings with which to propagate plants. Rhizomes are thick, fleshy roots that grow horizontally along the ground, or just under the soil. Periodically, they send up new shoots from along the length of the rhizome, spreading out the plant. Take rhizome cuttings when the plant is growing vigorously (usually in the late spring or early summer).

Dig up a section of rhizome and note that it grows in sections. The places where these sections join are called nodes. It is from these nodes that feeder roots (smaller stringy roots) extend downwards and new plants sprout upwards. You may even see that small plants are already sprouting. Cut the rhizome into pieces, with a node in each piece.

Fill a pot or planting tray to about 2.5 cm (1") from the top with perlite, vermiculite or seeding soil mix. Moisten the soil and let the excess water drain away. Lay the rhizome pieces flat on the top of the soil and almost cover them with more soil mix. If you leave a small bit of the top exposed to the light it will encourage the shoots to sprout. The soil mix does not have to be kept wet, but you should moisten it when it dries out to avoid having your rhizome rot. Once your cuttings have established themselves they can be potted individually and grow on in the same manner as the stem cuttings (see p. 28).

Oregano, thyme, rosemary, chives and flat-leaf parsley (left), hops (right)

Herbs to Propagate from Cuttings
Bergamot
Hops
Lemon Balm
Oregano/Marjoram
Rosemary
Scented Geranium
Soapwort
Tarragon

Division

Division is quite possibly the easiest way to propagate plants. Annuals, perennials and most tropical plants can be divided, but trees, shrubs or any woody ornamentals, including some vines, cannot be divided because they share a central stem or crown. If that central stem or crown is divided, all of the plant will fail.

Most plants form larger and larger clumps as they grow. Dividing this clump will rejuvenate the plant, keep its size in check and provide you with more plants. How often a plant can be divided will vary. Some plants need dividing almost every year to keep

them vigorous, while others can last a few years before dividing. You will know when a perennial should be divided if:
• the centre of the plant has died out
• the plant is no longer flowering as profusely as it did in previous years
• the plant is encroaching on the growing space of other plants in the bed.

Begin by digging up the entire plant and knocking any large clods of soil away from the root ball. The clump can then be split into several pieces. A small plant with fibrous roots can be torn into sections by hand. A large plant can be pried apart with a pair of garden forks inserted back to back into the clump. Plants with thicker tuberous or rhizomatous roots can be cut into sections with a sharp, sterile knife. In all cases, cut away any old sections that have died out and replant only the newer, more vigorous sections.

Once your original clump is divided into sections, replant one or two of them in the original location. Work organic matter into the soil before replanting. The other sections can be moved to new spots in the garden or potted up and given away. Get the sections back into the ground as quickly as possible to prevent the exposed roots from drying out. Put your plant divisions in pots if you aren't sure where to put them. Water new transplants thoroughly and keep them well watered until they have re-established themselves.

The larger the sections of the division, the more quickly the plant will re-establish itself and grow to blooming size again. Very small divisions may benefit from being planted in pots until they are bigger and better able to fend for themselves in the border.

Newly planted divisions will need extra care and attention when they are first planted. They will need regular watering and, for the first few days, shade from direct sunlight. A light covering of burlap or damp newspaper should be sufficient shelter for this short period. Move divisions that have been planted in pots to the shade.

Some gardeners prefer to divide plants while they are dormant, whereas others feel plants establish themselves more quickly if divided when they are growing vigorously. Experiment with dividing at different times of the year to see what works best. If you do divide plants while they are growing, you will need to cut back one-third to one-half of the growth so as not to stress the roots while they are repairing the damage done to them.

Herbs to Propagate by Division
Bee Balm
Calamint
Chamomile
Licorice
Lovage
Soapwort
Tarragon

If the plant you want to divide is not too large, a section of it can be divided off and replanted.

Pests and Diseases

Your garden may experience attacks from pests and diseases from time to time. There are numerous ways to deal with any problems that arise. Integrated Pest (or Plant) Management (IPM) is a moderate approach for dealing with pests and diseases. The goal of IPM is to reduce pest problems to levels of damage acceptable to you. Attempting to totally eradicate pests is futile. Consider whether a pest's damage is localized or covers the entire plant. Will the damage kill the plant, or is it only affecting the outward appearance? Can the pest be controlled without chemicals?

IPM includes learning about your plants and the conditions they need for healthy growth. It is also useful for you to learn what pests might affect your plants, where and when to look for those pests and how to control them. Keep records of pest damage because your observations can reveal patterns useful in spotting recurring problems and in planning your maintenance regime.

Prevention and Control

The first line of defence for your plants is to prevent pests and diseases from attacking in the first place. Provide the conditions necessary for healthy plant growth. Healthy plants are able to fend for themselves and can sustain some damage. Plants that are stressed or weakened are more subject to attack. Begin by choosing pest-resistant plants. Keep your soil healthy by using plenty of good-quality compost. Spray your plant's foliage with compost tea or fish emulsion, which acts as a foliar feed and also prevents fungal diseases.

Other cultural practices can help prevent pest attacks. Provide enough space for your plants so that they have good air circulation around them and are not stressed from competing for available resources. Remove plants that are decimated by pests and dispose of diseased foliage and branches. Keep your gardening tools clean and tidy up fallen leaves and dead plant matter in and around your permanently planted containers at the end of every growing season.

Physical controls are generally used to combat insect and mammal problems; for example, picking insects off plants by hand, which is easy if you catch the problem when it is just beginning. Large, slow insects are particularly easy to pick off. You can squish or rub off colonies of insects with your fingers. Other physical controls include traps, barriers, scarecrows and natural repellants that make a plant taste or smell bad to pests. Garden centres offer a wide array of such devices. Physical control of diseases usually involves removing the infected plant or parts of the plant to keep the problem from spreading.

Biological controls make use of populations of natural predators. Birds, spiders and many insects help keep pest populations at a manageable level. Encourage these creatures to take up permanent residence in or near your garden by planting appropriate food sources. Bird baths and feeders encourage birds to visit your garden and feed on a wide variety of insect pests. Many beneficial insects eat nectar from flowers.

Use chemical controls only as a last resort. Pesticide products can be either organic or synthetic. If you have tried the other suggested methods and still wish to take further action, try to use organic types, which are available at most garden centres.

Beneficial bugs: lacewing (top left), ladybug (centre), ladybug larvae (below).

Chemical or organic pesticides may also kill the beneficial insects you have been attracting. Many people think that because a pesticide is organic, they can use as much as they want. An organic spray kills because it contains a lethal toxin. NEVER overuse any pesticide. When using pesticides, follow the manufacturer's instructions carefully and apply in the recommended amounts only to the pests listed on the label. A large amount of pesticide is not any more effective in controlling pests than the recommended amount.

Caraway flowers attract beneficial insects.

What Now?

The herbs are planted and thriving in your garden outside and on your windowsill indoors, and they're all ready for harvest. Herbs are grown for a variety of purposes and for their different parts—their leaves, flowers, stems, roots, seeds and fruit. Some herbs may only have one "useful" part that is great for cooking and others are useful from top to bottom. A variety of ways exist to harvest and preserve the useful parts of the plant. These processes were commonly known in the 17th century but in many ways have become a lost art. Nowadays we can still take simple steps to use and preserve herbs.

The Harvest

For most herb gardeners, the delight is in the harvest. After a long season of growing, tending and care, the time finally arrives to collect the plant parts necessary to use throughout the year. Fortunately there's no magic moment when this all occurs, because most of the herbs recommended here produce leaves that are useful to the cook, artist and crafter. Leaves can be harvested all throughout the growing season, or all year-round when grown either in a climate that allows it or indoors. Flowers that are used fresh can also be picked throughout their blooming cycle.

There are no hard and fast rules when it comes to harvesting your herbs, you need to keep a few things in mind, such as when and how to pick them at their peak. First, depending on the size of the plant and how much lush growth is produced, pinch out growth for use on a regular basis. Don't take too much at a time: you will have to wait longer between harvests if you take more than 30–50 percent of the plant at once during the growing season. If a hard shearing is necessary to perk up the plant, go ahead—it won't hurt the plant's longevity. The plant will only reproduce what was taken away, time and energy allowing. If the growing season has come to an end, then you may want to cut the plant back to the base.

Pinching out the tips of branched plants encourages new growth as well as a bushier, denser growth habit. It can also enable the plant to divert some of its energy to other portions of the plant: for example, energy and nutrient storage in the roots, rhizomes or bulbs; flower, fruit and seed production; preparation for dormancy and awakening in the spring; and the production of the essential oils in every part of the plant.

The best time to harvest is when a plant's oil content is at its maximum. For most leafy herbs, this time is when the plant's flowers are just about to open. Mint is of one of the exceptions because the oils are at their maximum when the flowers are open completely. Usually seeds are harvested once they've turned colour, often from green to brown, usually in the fall. Seeds should be harvested before they fall to the ground, but only because it is much easier than trying to pick them out of the soil and before they begin to germinate. Roots are mostly harvested in the fall, once the growing season is finished. At this point, they're often fully developed and their storage is filled to capacity. Flowers vary somewhat as to when they should be harvested. For example, chamomile flowers should be picked when they're fully open, while others are better harvested just before they open and others are best picked just before they're open.

To harvest herbs throughout the growing season, make sure you have

Chopped curly-leaf parsley

sharp tools because dull blades may damage the plant or cause injuries to you. Pinch leaves from the tenderest parts of the plant, avoiding the woody portions, unless you plan on discarding them in the long run.

Morning is always the best time to harvest. Wait until the dew has evaporated but before it gets too hot. It's important to preserve the essential oils, and the hottest part of the day is when they're at their lowest. Remember the general rule: if the leaf is safe to eat then the flowers are as well. If the plant is in the midst of a blooming cycle, you may want to pick some of the flowers along with the leaves, for immediate or later use. Ideally, waiting an average of one two days after a thorough watering is also best, so the leaves are plump and bursting with essential oils. Place the stems in a little water and refrigerate for a few hours before cleaning and processing for storage, especially long term.

Herbs grown particularly for their edible flowers, such as nasturtiums, should only be picked immediately before you plan on preparing the meal. Freshly picked flowers don't store well and their flavours are at their best in early morning and late afternoon when the volatile oils are at their most concentrated. Rinse the flowers gently under tepid water, just as you would rinse the leaves, to remove any dirty residue or insects that may be tucked away. The flowers can also be soaked in water with a small amount of salt for about 15 minutes to ensure they're clean. Dry the flowers with a soft, dry towel or paper towel and refrigerate until needed. If you must cut the flowers several hours before serving them, treat them as you would fresh flowers for a bouquet. Keep the flowers on their stems and the stems in water, and refrigerate them until needed.

Collecting seeds is probably one of the easiest and fun parts of the harvest. Some seeds come encapsulated in a cover or remain on the inside the fruit, preventing the ripened seeds from escaping and falling to the ground. For plants with seeds that spill all over the ground once they've ripened, collect them before they drop. To prevent their escape, place a small, brown paper bag over the seed head shortly before the seeds ripen and turn brown to reddish brown, if not black. Gently cinch the mouth of the bag to the stem without cutting into the stem. Once the seeds have ripened and dried, cut the stem where the bag is attached and shake freely into the bag. If the seeds require a drying period, they can also be dried in the bag and stored in an airtight container later.

Harvesting roots is as simple as digging them up, and usually at the end of the season, particularly with annuals or plants grown as annuals. Remove the entire root of annuals when you're doing your fall clean-up. For hardy plants that you intend to leave in the ground, such as shrubs and perennials, remove only a part of the root and leave the rest. Remove no more than approximately one-third of the root to prevent shock to the plant. It will need at least two-thirds of the root to support the rest of the plant the following year. Gently rinse the soil from the root and let it dry for further processing. Don't be tempted to brush the soil from the root with a brush, because even the softest of bristles can damage the tender tissues you've so carefully grown.

Bulbs, such as onions and garlic, should be dug up either in late summer or early fall, depending on when you planted them.

A bumper crop of onions!

Potpourris with mint (left) and rose petals (right)

Processing and Preservation

One of the wonderful things about herbs is that so many can be dried, frozen or preserved in some way for later use. Each method is simple, and you'll be out in your garden harvesting, collecting and preserving your herbs in no time.

Drying Herbs

Drying herbs is probably the most common form of home preserving. It is important to ensure that all of the moisture is removed from the fresh leaves. A location with adequate to excellent air circulation is imperative, as is enough space to dry the herbs themselves. If mould sets in because the humidity is too high, the fresh material is still too wet. If the air is does not circulate, then your herbs are doomed. An average temperature to dry herbs at home is 20–32°C (68–90°F). To preserve the colour of your herbs, dry them in a dark place

You can dry herbs in the oven, particularly if you want to speed up the process. Most ovens are too hot to dry flowers and leaves even on their lowest settings, but they are well suited to drying roots. The microwave is another option for drying herbs but it's tricky because the heat causes the herbs to arc. To lessen this problem, place a small dish of water next to the herbs to boost the humidity— but the humidity can counteract drying herbs. Dehydrators are wonderful for drying leaves, flowers, fruit and seeds. Athough they can be expensive, a dehydrator is one of the best investments you can make if you plan to dry a lot of herbs over the years.

Air-drying is the easiest, least labour intensive and most successful process. Small-leaved green herbs can be left on their stems for drying, and larger-leaved herbs can be gently separated from the stems and left to dry spread out on screens, fabric or trays. Most gardeners collect a handful of leafy stems, tie their stems together in a bunch and hang them upside down until dry. This way is perfect for drying your leafy stems and

Chive flower

flowers. Drying racks, whether they're free standing or attached to the wall, are made for just this purpose and allow enough surface area to dry herbs.

Leave herbs until crackly dry to the touch. The length of time will differ from one herb to another, based on a variety of factors. Once dried, separate the bundles and gently strip the leaves from the stems. Larger leaves that have already been separated from the stems can be crumbled into pieces for storing.

Dried flowers can either be left in bundles for later use, if kept in an area where nothing can damage them, or they can be cut from their stems and stored.

Large flowerheads such as roses should be cut from their stems. The petals can be separated and loosely spread out onto paper or trays to dry. Some flowers can be dried whole, such as calendula. The petals can be separated later for use, once dried. Other flowers, such as lavender, are best dried in bunches, loosely tied with string. The flowerheads can be covered with

paper bags while drying to catch petals if they fall and to prevent them from getting dusty.

Depending on what you're using the flowers for, they can either be left intact once dry or stripped from their stems just as you would with the leaves. Some of the flowers can be dried upright, such as rosebuds and chive flowers. They're really only useful for decorative purposes and take up less space when dried in a base sturdy enough to support them.

Silica gels and specially treated dry sands for drying flowers are available at your local craft store. Using these products will better preserve the colour and shape of the flowers. These methods are only useful when preserving a few flowers, not large bunches.

Seeds are easiest to dry when you cut the stem with the flowerhead attached and store the entire cluster in a paper bag upside down until dry, shaking them loose later on. The paper bag method mentioned earlier is similar to this, and is best used on flowerheads that disperse their seeds too quickly. Once the seeds are dry, they should be stored in airtight containers and labelled.

Drying roots requires higher temperatures than flowers and leaves, around 50–60°C (120–140°F). Clean the roots, cut them into pieces and spread them out evenly on baking trays. Place the trays into a cool oven, with the door slightly open, then gradually turn the oven on to the lowest temperature setting to ensure even heat. Once the roots are brittle to the touch, take them out. Test the roots for doneness frequently—you don't want them to become browned or shriveled. The time it takes to dry the roots varies based on your oven, region and the moisture content and size of the root pieces.

Storing Dried Herbs

Airtight containers are the best method of storing dried herbs. Glass and wooden containers, airtight tins and paper bags are preferable to plastic ones. Plastic tends to encourage mould if there is a small amount of moisture left in the herbs. Dark and cool areas are the best places to store your herbs to preserve their oils, colours and flavours.

Frozen herbs can be used in any dishes that call for fresh or dried herbs.

For short-term storage, place leafy stems in between two layers of foil and refrigerate or place in a freezer bag and they will last 6–8 weeks.

For long-term storage, rinse freshly cut herbs in cold water and shake off any excess water. Remove the leaves from the tougher, older stems (unless it's a herb that has a useful stem), but leave tender young stems attached. Finely chop the herbs and pack into ice-cube trays. Top up with water and put in the freezer. Once frozen, put the frozen herb cubes into freezer bags for later use. Don't forget to label the bags, because the herbs can last 6–12 months when stored this way, and you're bound to forget what they are. The herb cubes can be used directly from the freezer to season soups, stews, casseroles and other dishes.

Herb-infused Oils and Vinegars

Preserving the flavours of herbs in vinegars and vegetable and olive oils is easy, and you can use these herbs in cooking, cosmetics and crafts. Herbal oils and vinegars can preserve a single flavour, such as basil, or a mixture of flavours, such as basil, oregano and thyme. Use three herbs or less per bottle; otherwise, the oil may become cloudy. Dishes including pasta, vegetables and meat will all benefit from the

Safflowers in oil

Some people dip the leaves of their herbs in oil before placing them between layers of foil before freezing. Oil isn't necessary and can cause the leaves to become soggy once thawed.

flavours and herbal perfumes preserved in oil or vinegar. Handmade herbal soaps and bath products are ideal for the fragrant oils in herbs such as rosemary.

It's important always to use a good quality, mild-flavoured oil such as sunflower or safflower oil. The goal is to preserve the flavour of the herb and not the oil. Olive oil is only suitable for strongly flavoured herbs or when a subtle herb flavour is desired. Cover the herbs completely by the oil during the infusing process, and remove all plant material from the container before storing it long-term.

Tarragon vinegar

Cold-infused Oils

Cold-infused oils should be prepared in a clean, sterilized container, preferably glass. Add a handful of herbs to the container, crushing them slightly as they enter the container to release their essential oils. Pour the oil into the container until the herbs are completely covered. Cover the container and stand it in a warm location such as a sunny windowsill. Shake the container daily. After a week or so, strain the herbs from the oil and replace with another batch of the same herb or herbs. Leave for another week to further infuse the flavours. This process can be repeated until the flavour is to your liking, then remove the herbs from the oil and pour the oil into a clean, sterilized container with an airtight lid. The oil will keep for a period of weeks to months. Keep the oil in a dark, cool location to ensure its longevity. Make small batches of infused oil until you to know how often you use it. You don't want stagnant or rancid oil that you weren't able to finish using, and smaller batches will always leave you with freshly flavoured oil.

Heat-infused Oils

Heat-infused oils are prepared by placing a ceramic or glass bowl over a pot of simmering water, just as you would melt chocolate. Pour the desired amount of oil into the bowl, and stir in your choice of fresh herbs. Let the mixture stand over low heat for up to three hours. Once cooled, strain out the bits and pour the oil into a dark-coloured, sterilized bottle, seal tightly and store in a cool, dark place.

Infused vinegars can be prepared in the same way as oils. Infused herbal vinegars can be made with fresh, dried or frozen herbs. Flower petals, seeds, bulbs leaves and fruit can be added to vinegar just as they can be added into light oils. Savory herbal vinegars, such as tarragon vinegar, are fantastic when used on salads, while fruity vinegars add sharpness and a hint of sweetness to vegetable dishes. Fruit vinegars, such as one infused with raspberry, also work well to relieve a sore throat, and a compress wet with lavender vinegar can relieve a headache when applied to the forehead. Herbal vinegars often have antiseptic qualities.

Some homemade cosmetics call for a base of cider vinegar, which is said to restore the acid mantle of the skin. It is traditionally used in homemade hair rinses and skin lotions. Vinegars made with rose petals or a mixture of mint and marigold are great when diluted in water and used as facial toners. Because vinegar does not spoil as quickly as oil, you can make herbal vinegars in larger batches.

Preserving Herbs in Sugar

Sugar is an excellent medium for herbs and is useful in a variety of dishes, particularly desserts. Edible flowers can be crystallized in sugar by simply painting the petals with a thin coat of lightly whipped egg whites and covering them in caster or super fine sugar. The crystallized flowers are then spread out on a baking tray and placed into an oven on the lowest setting, only until completely dry and brittle, but not brown. They'll keep in airtight containers in the fridge or freezer for weeks if not months.

Sugar infused with the flavours of herbs such as lavender is a sweet addition to cakes, biscuits and cookies. It's worth having a small container of it on hand if you bake often. To create lavender sugar, simply add lavender flower spikes to some sugar, sieve the flowers from the sugar once the flavour is to your liking and store in an airtight container.

Herbal Honey

Herbs can also be preserved in honey. Choose the finest honey you can find and add your favourite herbs to a small quantity of honey in an airtight container. Once infused, the honey can be drizzled into herbal teas for a unique flavour or taken in teaspoonfuls to alleviate sore throats and cold symptoms.

Herbed Butter

Herbed butter is a tasty way to add flavour to many dishes. Savory breads and herbed butters are ideal matches, as are sandwiches, biscuits and scones. Herbed butter can be melted over a steaming cob of corn or just about any cooked vegetable. You can create all kinds of herb mixtures for butter, just as you would for herbal oils and vinegars; it just depends on your taste.

Dried and fresh sage, and sage butter

You'll have to experiment with the ratio of herbs to butter, but the general recommendation is 2–3 tbsp (30–45 ml) of finely chopped, fresh herbs for every 1lb (454 g) of softened butter. You can also add edible flowers for colour and flavour, and lemon juice and pepper to taste if you like. Once mixed, roll the butter into a log and wrap it in a layer or two of plastic wrap or wax paper. Refrigerate until firm enough to slice into pats. Alternatively, pipe the butter into "kisses" onto a baking sheet and refrigerate for a couple of hours or until firm. The butter pats or kisses can be stored in airtight bags or containers in the refrigerator for up to three months. The combinations are limited only by your imagination.

What to Do with Your Herbs

Now that they're preserved, what creations can you whip up with your herbs? The culinary options are endless. There are few recipes that don't call for at least one herb, and even when they call for a particular herb, you may find that you prefer another or a combination of two or three to enhance the flavours of the dish.

Textile artists, dyers, spinners and crafters have been using herbs as natural dyes for centuries and for good reason. Natural dyes are non-toxic, easy to use, offer a range of beautiful colours and can be grown in your own backyard. Safflower flower petals offer warm yellow hues, as do tansy and other herbs with brightly coloured flowers and foliage.

Use dyes and herbs in handmade toiletries such as soaps, lotions, hair rinses, cosmetics. Dyes lend warm colour while herbs enhance fragrance, colour and aromatherapeutic and homeopathic properties. Herbs can also improve the texture and colour of handmade products such as candles, soaps and paper.

Once you've decided what to do with your treasured herbs, you'll find yourself experimenting more and more, trying to perfect your crafts, dishes and the environment around you. When we connect with the natural world, surrounding ourselves with plants and all the things they can be used to create, we find ourselves living more healthily and with a closer connection to nature, something that has been lost over the generations.

Have fun growing and nurturing your herbs. Enjoy everything they have to offer and treat all of your successes and failures as a part of a learning experience, because there is no right and wrong, only something to build upon.

The Language of Herbs

Herbs, particularly in the Victorian era, were used to represent different emotions and to symbolically communicate the heart's desires. Many of the meanings remain the same today, but without the scandalous intrigue.

Basil, for example, represents fidelity or love, whereas lavender means distrust. Lemon balm in an arrangement represents sympathy, and yarrow says "healing of the heart." Marjoram represents happiness, borage says courage and rosemary symbolizes remembrance.

Recipes and Craft Suggestions

Rose and Lemon Potpourri

3 tbsp (45 ml) orrisroot, premixed with 15 drops of rose oil

2 cups (500 ml) dried rosebuds and rose petals

1 cup (250 ml) dried rose-scented geranium leaves

1 cup (250 ml) dried lemon verbena

Combine the orrisroot and rose oil in a glass jar, screw the lid on tightly and shake well. Mix the remaining ingredients together and pour into the jar. Shake well again. Transfer into an airtight container and leave to infuse for at least two weeks. Remove what it is needed into a decorative dish or bowl and keep the remaining mixture in the airtight container for later use.

Dream Pillows

Dream Pillows or sweet pillows are sachets or packets of herbs tucked between the pillow and pillowcase. The aroma released from the herbs supposedly improves sleep and may even help shape your dreams. Chamomile flowers are said, for example, to dispel nightmares and calendula flowers to promote auspicious dreams. Combining rose petals, lavender flowers and leaves and lemon verbena leaves produces a calming and soothing scent used in aromatherapy to assist in deep, restful sleep and stress reduction. To induce deep sleep, combine hops and chamomile flowers, peppermint and lavender leaves. The herbal packet or sachet can also be placed between the fitted sheet and mattress or hung from the headboard to prevent waking light sleepers.

Sachets

Sachets used purely for their fragrance are easy to make and can be used to scent just about anything, such as closets, trunks, rooms, suitcases or cars. What you choose to include in your sachet is up to you. A small pocket of linen or cotton, approximately the size of your palm, is ideal for stuffing with your favourite scented herbs. Finish it off with a strip of ribbon to put it wherever you desire a hit of fragrance.

Wreaths

Herbal wreaths, tussie mussies and herbal ropes are useful wherever you would like to add a little fragrance, but rather than hiding them away, these treasures can be. Lavender wreaths are lovely and add a delicate touch to a bedroom or. The steam from a bath or shower will help to bring out the essential oils of the leaves and flowers. Catnip is also another ideal herb for this purpose. Its flexible stems can be braided together, either alone or combined with other herbs, and used to scent vanities, wardrobes—even your cubicle at the office. Many herbs also possess natural insecticidal properties and help ward off moths and other critters that may harm your clothes.

Therapeutic, natural preparations for toiletries, bath products and cosmetics have made a huge comeback because of the known adverse affects of synthetic ingredients and chemical preservatives. What you apply to your body is as important as what you put into your body. The following are a few simply made products that you can integrate into your daily routine, and use to replace products harmful to you and the environment.

Rosewater Toner

⅔ cup (150 ml) rosewater

⅔ cup (150 ml) witch hazel

6 drops glycerin

Combine all of the ingredients into a container with a lid and shake before use. Use as a facial skin toner after washing, to refresh and invigorate the skin before moisturizing, particularly before bed.

Lip Balm

Combine two to three drops or more of lemon verbena, thyme, lavender, scented geranium, jasmine and peppermint or other essential oils you prefer, to 1 tbsp (15 ml) of warmed cocoa butter. Mix and transfer into a small jar, allowing it to cool. Once cool, apply a thin layer to the lips when dry.

Foot Bath

Sprinkle handfuls of individual portions of fresh bay leaves, lavender, thyme, lemon balm, marjoram and spearmint, or combinations thereof into a large bowl, with 2 tsp (10 ml) of salt and enough hot water to cover the feet and ankles. Submerge your tired feet into the hot water for at least 10 minutes for a soothing treat.

Lavender Spritz

Place a couple of drops of lavender oil into a small atomizer or spray bottle, with enough distilled water to fill the container. Shake to blend and spritz onto your face for an invigorating skin freshener.

Invigorating Herbal Bath

Add 2 tbsp (30 ml) each of sage, strawberry leaf and mint to a hot bath and soak for 20 minutes, drawing in the sweet aroma as the essential oils are released from the herbs onto your skin. Another ideal combination for a rejuventating and calming bath is 2 tbsp (30 ml) each of calendula petals, lavender, sweet marjoram, mint or rosemary.

Stimulating Marigold Bath

Add 1 cup (250 ml) of dried marigold petals and 1 tsp (5 ml) of baby oil into a warm, not hot, bath. Soak for at least 15 minutes. This combination is said to possess dehydrating properties and act as an astringent.

Chamomile facial bath in sink (above), sorrel leaves can be steeped to create a facial bath (below)

Wild Garden Shower Soap

½ cup (125 ml) distilled water
½ cup (125 ml) orange flower water
1 tbsp (15 ml) dried peppermint leaves
1 tbsp (15 ml) dried chamomile
1 tbsp (15 ml) dried rose petals
1 tbsp (15 ml) orange blossoms
½ tbsp (7.5 ml) unscented glycerin soap
1 tsp (5 ml) castor oil

Combine the distilled water and orange flower water in a saucepan and bring to a boil. Remove the pan from the heat and add the dried peppermint, chamomile, rose petals and orange blossoms. Let steep for 1 hour. Strain the herbs and flowers from the water and reheat gently. Add the glycerin soap and stir in the castor oil. Let cool to room temperature and bottle. This shower soap is mild enough for everyday use.

Herbal Oatmeal Soap

This soothing soap is a great way to reconnect with nature through skin-loving herbs and oatmeal. It's great for dry skin and is easy to make with melt-and-pour soap you can purchase at any craft store. It yields approximately 17, 4oz (28 g) bars, depending on the size of the moulds, and takes about 1–2 hours to make, including cooling time.

1 lb (454 g) melt-and-pour soap base
¼ tsp (1.25 ml) rosemary essential oil
¼ tsp (1.25 ml) sage essential oil
¼ tsp (1.25 ml) lavender essential oil
1 cup (250 ml) oatmeal
¼ cup (62.5 ml) dried chamomile flowers
¼ cup (62.5 ml) calendula petals
⅛ cup (30 ml) dried rosemary
⅛ cup (30 ml) dried rose hips
1½ cups (375 ml) distilled water

Combine the water, oatmeal and herbs in a saucepan. Heat to boiling, then cover and let simmer a minimum of 30 minutes. Let cool, covered. When the mixture is cool enough to handle, strain it through a double or triple folded cheesecloth. Set aside. The resulting thick liquid is a slurry. Using a sharp knife, cut your melt-and-pour soap base into 1 inch (2.5 cm) cubes and place in a microwave-safe measuring bowl. Microwave on high for 30 seconds at a time, stirring periodically until the base is nearly melted. Remove and stir until all soap base pieces have melted. If you don't have a microwave oven, melt the soap in a double-boiler. Stir the base slowly and minimally to prevent any air bubbles. Handle the hot liquid with great care and let it cool down before you add the essential oils or the scents will vaporize. Add the herbal slurry and essential oils as soon as you can comfortably touch the mixture. Stir gently and pour into moulds. Allow the soap to stand until it hardens. Place the moulds into the freezer for 10 or 15 minutes or until the mixture is firm. Once the soap has hardened, it is easier to get out of the moulds. The bars can be used immediately and will last for 6–12 months.

Basic Savory Herbal Infused Oil

4 tbsp (60 ml) fresh, chopped herbs, either all of one kind or a combination
2 cups (500 ml) of light oil, such as olive, sunflower or safflower

Crush the herbs and transfer into a bowl. Add the oil slowly. Coat the herbs with the oil and pour into a container with an airtight lid. Keep at room temperature for at least 2 weeks while the oils from the herbs infuse into the oil. Strain the herbs out of the oil and transfer the flavoured oil into a jar or bottle.

Basic Herbal Infused Vinegar

2 cups (500 ml) white wine vinegar
4 sprigs of culinary herbs, sized to fit bottle, or 2 tbsp (30 ml) herb seeds such as fennel, coriander or dill

Pour the vinegar into a decorative, airtight bottle, until it reaches about 3 inches (7.5 cm) from the top. Add the herbal sprigs or seeds to the vinegar and seal with a lid or cap. Leave the bottle to infuse at room temperature for 2 weeks. Once infused, strain out the herbs or seeds and replace with fresh ones for a more intense flavour. Store the infused vinegar in the refrigerator.

Fragrant Thai Oil

2 stalks lemongrass, halved lengthwise
6 kaffir lime leaves or lime zest
2 slices fresh ginger
1 tiny red chili pepper
2 ½ (750 ml) cups sunflower oil

Lightly crush the ingredients and transfer into a wide-necked bottle. Fill with the sunflower oil and leave to infuse for up to 2 weeks. Store in a cool place when not in use. This spicy oil is ideal for drizzling over steamed fish or to enhance marinades. It also makes a tasty dip for salad rolls when mixed with rice vinegar.

Fennel and Lemon Butter

1 stick (100 g) lightly salted, softened butter

2 tbsp (30 ml) chopped fennel leaves

grated zest of half a lemon

freshly ground pepper to taste

Combine the butter, fennel, lemon zest and pepper in a bowl and beat until evenly mixed. Smooth mixture onto plastic wrap and roll into a 1–2 inch (2.5–5 cm) wide log and chill until firm. Once firm, cut into pats and serve with fish or cooked vegetables. It is also quite tasty when sprinkled over popcorn.

Bouquet Garni and Fines Herbes

A *bouquet garni* is a bundle of herbs added to dishes such as stews and soups. Often this bundle includes parsley, marjoram, thyme and bay leaf. Basil, chervil, tarragon and salad burnet can be used, depending on the flavours desired. Herbs in a *bouquet garni* are tied together at the stem, enclosed in a cheesecloth bag and left to steep in the pot until the food is cooked. Remove the bag before serving the dish.

Fines herbes differ in that the herbs are finely chopped and sprinkled over the dish prior to cooking, and they are not removed before serving. Parsley is often the main herb used in French cooking, and specifically flat-leaf parsley if cooking in the Italian style. To many North American cooks, *fines herbes* is a

combination of chopped parsley, tarragon, chives and chervil. Other possibilities include rosemary, sage, marjoram, basil and oregano.

Poor Man's Capers (Pickled Nasturtium Seedpods)

green nasturtium seedpods

2 cups (500 ml) water

1 tbsp (15 ml) salt

garlic cloves, peeled

pickling spices

white wine vinegar, enough to fill jars

pickling jars, size of your choice

Soak green seedpods for 24 hours in a brine made from the water and salt. Drain. Pack small, sterilized jars with the drained seedpods. Include 1 peeled clove of garlic and 1 tsp (5 ml) of pickling spices in each jar. Heat white wine vinegar to simmering and fill each jar with the vinegar. Seal with acid-proof lids and let the seedpods sit for about a month. Eat pickled seedpods within a week of opening.

About this Guide

The plants featured here are organized alphabetically by their most common familiar names. Additional common names appear in the Features section of each entry. This system enables you to find a plant easily if you are familiar with only the common name. The scientific or botanical name is always listed after the common name. I encourage you to learn these botanical names. Several plants may share the same common name, and they vary from region to region. Only the specific botanical name identifies the specific plant anywhere in the world.

Clearly indicated within each entry are the plant's height and spread ranges, outstanding features and hardiness zone(s), if applicable. Each entry gives clear instructions for planting and growing the plants, and recommends many of our favourite selections. If height and spread ranges or hardiness zones are not given for every recommended plant, assume these ranges are the same as those provided in the Features section. Your local garden centre will have any additional information about the plant and will help you make your plant selections.

Finally, the Pests and Diseases section of the introduction deals with issues that afflict you garden plants from time to time.

Anise

Pimpinella

Anise has a wide variety of culinary uses, including in salads, desserts, candy and baked delicacies. Throughout history, the licorice scent of anise has been used in fragrances, liqueurs, cosmetics and even pharmaceutical products. This versatile herb may have fallen out of favour in our modern kitchens, but it is deserving of a place on your windowsill or in your garden, pantry, medicine cabinet and vanity.

Features

Other names: aniseed
Parts used: leaves, seeds and oil
Hardiness: half-hardy annual

Growing

Anise prefers **well-drained, rich or fertile, moist** and **sandy** soil. **Neutral to slightly alkaline** soil and **partial shade to full sun** are ideal. A location sheltered from wind will prevent the seeds from broadcasting themselves everywhere.

Grow anise from seed indoors in early spring or directly into the soil in late spring, depending on your zone's last frost dates.

Companion plant anise next to coriander/cilantro because its seeds will germinate more quickly if sown near coriander seed. Sow the seeds thickly so that the plants will help to support each other.

Tips

Because of its taproot, anise dislikes being transplanted. It grows well in a container or in the garden, as long as it is not moved. You'll likely need several anise plants to harvest a useful crop of seed, so grow it in the garden if you plan to collect seeds.

Recommended

P. anisum is a half-hardy annual that grows roughly 18–24" (46–60 cm) tall and 12" (30 cm) wide. The fragrant leaves are bolder, larger and more prominent toward the base of the plant, but feathery, delicate and flattish toward the tips of the stems. White flowerheads bloom in mid- to late summer and are produced in an umbel form similar to dill. Aromatic, licorice-scented, small, brown seeds or fruit forms once the flowers are spent.

Anise flowers

Harvesting and Processing

Once flowers are full of mature, brown seeds, cut the flowerheads off, place them in cardboard boxes, paper bags or on sheets of paper in a sunny, dry location to remove any moisture. Rub dried flowers between the palms of your hands to remove the seeds, and store them in an airtight container to preserve them.

Uses

Anise is most commonly used to make tea, but whole or ground seeds also taste wonderful in quick breads. Anise complements other flavours, and the seeds help in digesting such foods as pasta, cooked apples or pears, cabbage, carrots, beetroot and bread. This herb is frequently used in Indian and Moroccan cuisine and in cookies and other desserts.

Anise oil can be used topically as a fragrant antiseptic or in scented soaps, massage oils and handmade lotions.

Because anise seeds contain anethole, a plant hormone similar to human estrogen, women who are pregnant or nursing should avoid them.

Arugula

Eruca

Some consider this plant to be a vegetable while others think it's a herb, and they're both right. This peppery flavoured plant is native to parts of Asia and southern Europe, but is only naturalized in parts of North America. It is relatively well known and has experienced waves of popularity over the years. After close to two centuries of being overlooked, arugula is experiencing a new life in Canada. In fact, it's become quite fashionable, trendy even. It deserves such accolades, but I'd like to see it used in everyday cooking more often by the public rather than only in fancy bistros and restaurants, because it has so much to offer.

Arugula combines well with other herbs, including parsley, lovage, cilantro, basil, cresses, dill, borage and salad burnet.

Arugula salad and seeds

Features
Other names: salad rocket, roquette, rucola
Parts used: leaves, flowers, seeds
Hardiness: annual

Growing
Arugula prefers to grow in **full to partial sun**. **Cool, moist** and **rich** soil will help to produce more tender and less pungent leaves than dry, hot soil. Wait to sow seed until the risk of frost has passed. It can be started from seed, in succession, throughout the growing season. Successively seeding crops will provide you with young, tender leaves all summer. Arugula is known to self-seed prolifically.

Tips
Arugula is best grown either in a vegetable or herb garden setting. The leaves, although attractive, don't have much to offer aesthetically. Arugula doesn't lend itself well to container growing and is best grown in the ground outdoors. However, it is possible to grow arugula in pots. Make sure to sow the seed early in spring and use a bark/compost potting mix. Pinch the new leaves out frequently for use and maintain a good level of moisture without keeping the soil too wet. Be careful not to fertilize excessively because this results in lush leaves that lack flavour.

Recommended
E. vesicaria subsp. *sativa* is an upright annual with toothed leaves on tall stems tipped with four-petalled flowers in white, veined with purple, reminiscent of scented geranium flowers. Slender, erect seed pods follow after the flowers. It grows 24–36" (60–90 cm) tall but only 6–8" (15–20 cm) wide.

Arugula grows best in full sun

Harvesting and Processing

The tender leaves are best when picked before the flower stems emerge because they become more pungent and somewhat bitter over time. The leaves are ready for harvest six to eight weeks after sowing. They should always be used fresh, because drying them diminishes their flavour. Arugula does not freeze well.

Uses

Popular in Mediterranean cuisine, the peppery leaves of arugula are mainly used as a salad herb and are commonly found in mesclun, a mixture of salad greens originating in southern France, around Nice. When used in salads, arugula combines well with nutty oil dressings. The leaves can also be added to stir-fries, pasta sauces, potato salad or almost any dish where spinach is used. Arugula is particularly tasty in egg dishes; poached eggs are delicious when set atop a bed of arugula leaves. It also blends beautifully with prosciutto, with mushrooms and with mild cheeses in sandwiches and hors d'oeuvres. Herbal butters,

Arugula in bloom (above and top right)

dressings and pesto, with or without basil, also benefit from arugula's lightly piquant flavour.

Arugula was once thought to have many medicinal qualities, but is now only really used as a culinary herb.

The flowers, seeds and an oil extract are also edible. The flowers, which taste citrusy, can be used as an edible garnish.

You may come across a plant called wild arugula, which is completely different from the one recommended here. Wild arugula, *Diplotaxis muralis*, is a perennial that produces leaves that are more ornate than, but just as pungent as, those of *Eruca vesicaria*. Turkish arugula, *Bunias orientalis*, produces leaves that resemble those of a dandelion.

The leaves are aromatic, producing a peppery scent as they are harvested.

Leaves taste more peppery as they age, but leaf flavour diminishes almost entirely once the flowers appear.

Harvested arugula leaves

Basil

Ocimum

Of any herb, basil is probably the one that has been grown by every level of green thumb. There is an amazing array to choose from in the basil family, and new introductions are revealed almost annually. The fragrant leaves of fresh basil add a delicious flavour to a wide variety of savoury and sweet dishes, so it's no surprise that it is one of the mainstays of cooking today.

Basil flowers and leaves

Features
Parts used: leaves, seeds and oil
Hardiness: annual

Growing
Basil grows best in a **warm, sheltered** location in **full sun**. The soil should be **fertile, moist** and **well drained**. Pinch tips regularly to encourage bushy growth. Remove all flower spikes and fertilize with an organic fertilizer, like compost tea. You'll soon see a fresh crop of growth emerge.

Starting basil from seed can be a challenge, but if you're determined to try, start the seed indoors so that you can plant the seedlings out in the spring after any risk of frost has passed, or start with young plants purchased from your local garden centre.

Tips
Though basil will grow best in a warm spot outdoors in the garden, it can be grown successfully in a pot by a bright window indoors to provide you with fresh leaves all year.

Recommended
O. basilicum is a very frost-sensitive annual. Although there are many species, hybrids and cultivars to choose from, the tender leaves are easily damaged by both frost and lengthy periods of intense, direct sun. It produces aromatic, lush green and sometimes purple-flushed foliage in a bushy form, 12–24" (30–60 cm) tall and 12–18" (30–46 cm) wide. Purple- or pink-tinged flowers are produced in spikes above the foliage. The following are only a small sample of what is available: **'Ararat'** bears purple-marked foliage with a strong hint of anise flavour; **'Cinnamon'** has a clean, spicy aroma with a hint of cinnamon, and distinctly veined foliage and purple-stained stems; **'Compatto'** is a compact form of **'Genovese'** and both are standard large-leaf selections and very flavourful; **Var. minimum** (bush basil,

O. basilicum 'Red Rubin' (above), basil seeds (below)

Greek basil) is a dwarf selection with tiny, pungent leaves and white flowers; **'Magical Michael,'** a 2002 AAS recipient, bears red-veined foliage and stems, with a fruity aroma and burgundy flowers; **'Mini Purpurescens Wellsweep'** forms a mound of dark purple foliage edged in bright green; **'Pistou'** grows to 8" (20 cm) tall in a bushy, dwarf form; **'Purple Ruffles'** is another AAS winner with large, heavily ruffled and fringed, dark purple foliage and pink flowers; **'Siam Queen,'** the 1997 AAS winner, bears dark purple flowers atop dark

green leaves, with a spicy licorice flavour; **'Special Select'** is one of the best basils for pesto, bearing bright green leaves; **'Spicy Globe'** is a uniform bush basil with larger leaves; and **'Sweet Dani,'** yet another AAS winner, produces the strongest lemon flavour and scent available on the market.

Harvesting and Processing

To use fresh basil in the kitchen, pinch out the newest tips throughout the growing season for cooking. As fall approaches, closely watch the weather forecasts and ensure that you have cut the leafy stalks down for drying indoors long before a fall frost. Bunches can be air dried and stored in an airtight container; however, there is the possibility that mould could set in if the leaves take too long to dry. The leaves can be chopped finely, mixed with a little water and frozen into ice cubes for cooking.

If you choose to take your pots of basil indoors to use through the

O. basilicum, flowering (above), *O. basilicum* 'Siam Queen' (below)

colder months, make sure to pinch the newest growth back often to promote a stalky, bushy plant. Place your basil in a location with as much natural light as possible or under an artificial growing light.

Uses

Basil is used mostly for culinary purposes including soups, breads, casseroles, dips, spreads and so on. It's also very prevalent in certain cuisines, including Thai and Mediterranean. Cosmetic and medical uses are possible, but limited.

Basil is a good companion plant for tomatoes—both like warm, moist growing conditions and when you pick tomatoes for a salad, you'll also remember to include a few leaves of basil.

Not all types of basil are suitable for cooking because they may be too strong or bitter, overwhelming a dish rather than complementing it.

Bay Laurel

Laurus

Bay laurel is positively one of the easiest herbs to grow. Its refined appearance and form is ideally suited to formal settings when trained and used as topiary in decorative containers. It's an undemanding plant that is happily transferred from a sunny window indoors to a lightly shaded spot outdoors when the weather allows.

In ancient Greece and Rome, victorious athletes and soldiers were crowned with bay laurel wreaths.

Features
Other names: bay, sweet bay, Grecian bay
Parts used: leaves
Hardiness: zones 8–10 (grown mostly as an annual throughout Canada)

Growing
Bay laurel grows well in **light shade, partial shade** or **full sun**, in **moist** and **well drained** soil in a sheltered location. Fertilize monthly with half-strength fertilizer. Because bay laurel is a woody plant, starting from seed isn't recommended. Start with young plants grown in containers, which are easy to move inside for the winter.

Tips
Bay laurel is an attractive, small shrub that is useful as a structural point in a mixed container or as a specimen. Pinch it back to maintain a compact form or train it as a standard. Combine it with other herbs in themed containers.

Recommended
L. nobilis is an aromatic, evergreen tree or shrub that grows 12–36" (30–60 cm) tall and 12–24" (30–60 cm) wide, but can reach 40' (12 m) heights where it is hardy. In a container it stays much smaller and can be pruned to maintain a suitable size. **'Angustifolia'** (willowleaf bay) has narrow, wavy-edged, pale green foliage, while **'Aurea'** has golden yellow foliage.

Harvesting and Processing
Bay leaves are familiar to most of us as the large, flat leaves we pick out of our stews or soups before serving. To dry the leaves, pick them from the stems and spread them out on a wire rack, where they will dry quickly, retaining their colour.

Naturally dried and freeze-dried bay leaves

Branches with leaves attached can also be hung in a dark, airy place.

Uses
The culinary uses for bay laurel are enormous. Many cooks find the leaves indispensable in many types of cuisines and dishes. Individual leaves are an essential ingredient in a *bouquet garni*, a spray of herbs that includes parsley, marjoram, thyme and a few peppercorns used to flavour soups and stews, and which is removed after cooking.

Bay laurel leaves can be added to a facial steam bath containing a combination of other herbs, depending on your skin type. Chamomile flowers, rosemary, rose petals and bay laurel leaves are perfect for normal skin types. Dried bay laurel leaves can be used in potpourri blends and added to sleep pillows for insomnia. Crafters have traditionally used bay laurel branches for wreaths and swags.

Bergamot

Monarda

Bergamot has a bit of a bad reputation for developing powdery mildew, but planting newer, mildew-resistant varieties and ensuring ample air circulation around the plant will help prevent this problem. The recommended section lists the most mildew-resistant varieties currently available. Among bergamot's assets are its abundant flowers, which attract all kinds of nectar-loving bugs and birds, and its lemon-scented leaves, which can be used to brew tea.

A refreshing bergamot facial steam bath

Features

Other names: bee balm
Parts used: leaves, flowers
Hardiness: zones 3–8

Growing

Bergamot grows well in **full sun**, **partial shade** or **full shade**. The soil should be of **average fertility, humus rich, moist** and **well drained**. Divide every two or three years in spring before new growth emerges.

To help prevent powdery mildew, thin stems in spring to increase air circulation. Plant in full sun; partial to heavy shade increases the possibility that mildew will form. If mildew strikes after flowering, cut the infected portions out, back to the healthy growth, to about 6" (15 cm), and new flowers and healthy foliage will re-emerge.

This plant is named after the Spanish botanist and physician Nicholas Monardes (1493–1588).

Tips

Use bergamot beside a stream or pond, or in a lightly shaded, well-watered border.

Bergamot will attract bees, butterflies and hummingbirds to your garden. Avoid using pesticides that can seriously harm or kill these creatures, especially if you plan to ingest this, or any plant, in your garden.

Recommended

M. didyma is a bushy, mounding plant that forms a thick clump of stems. It grows 2–4' (61 cm–1.2 m) tall and spreads 12–24" (30–61 cm). Red or pink flowers are borne in late summer. **'Gardenview Scarlet'** bears large scarlet flowers and is resistant to powdery mildew. **'Marshall's Delight'** doesn't come true to type from seed and must be propagated by cuttings or divisions. It is very resistant to powdery mildew and bears pink flowers. **'Panorama'** is a group of hybrids with flowers in scarlet, pink or salmon. **'Petite Delight'**

Bergamot tea (above), *M. didyma* (below)

is the first in a series of dwarf varieties. It grows to 12–18" (30–46 cm) tall and bears purply pink flowers. **'Raspberry Wine'** bears red wine–coloured flowers. **'Rosy Purple'** reaches 3–4' (90 cm–1.2 m) heights and has deep purple red flowers; **'Violet Queen'** grows equally tall and bears deep purple flowers.

Harvesting and Processing

The leaves and flowers should be harvested for drying in late summer when the plant is in full bloom. Spread the flowers and leaves out on a wire rack in a shady, airy location and store when dry in an airtight container. Fresh bergamot leaves and flowers can be minced and mixed with water for freezing in ice cube trays.

M. didyma (all photos this page)

Uses

The fresh or dried leaves may be used to make a refreshing, minty, citrus-scented tea. Put a handful of fresh leaves in a teapot, pour boiling water over the leaves and let steep for at least five minutes. Sweeten the tea with honey to taste. The leaves can be added to salads, cooling summer beverages, vegetable dishes, sweet jellies and even pork and veal dishes. Fresh or dried, the leaves can be used interchangeably with mint for a switch.

Cosmetically, bergamot can be used in a hot bath to perfume the water. Crafters frequently use the dried leaves in potpourri and their essence for bath oils, soaps and lotions.

As one of its names suggests, bee balm is extremely attractive to bees, as well as hummingbirds and other pollinators. It's also a nectar source for butterflies.

Borage

Borago

Borage is a vigorous, tenacious annual herb. It is valued by some but disliked by others because of its natural inclination to reseed itself everywhere. The flowers and foliage are not only pretty, but also delicious when used in salads, desserts, tea and sweet and cold beverages.

Use only small amounts of borage leaves when cooking because they contain a compound that could be toxic if consumed in large quantities.

Features
Other names: cool-tankard, talewort, bee bread
Parts used: flowers, leaves
Hardiness: zones 5–10

Growing
Borage prefers **full sun** but will also thrive in **partial shade. Moist**, **sandy**, **well-drained** soil is best. Borage is drought tolerant once established. Remove any unwanted seedlings as they emerge in early spring to prevent an onslaught of plants.

Tips
Plant borage in your vegetable or herb garden to attract bees for pollination. As an ornamental, it contrasts beautifully with dark foliage specimens. Borage will grow with wild abandon in dry, hot areas where little else will grow.

Recommended
B. officinalis is an upright plant with high clusters of pendent, violet blue, star-shaped flowers in spring. The stems and foliage are covered in silvery hairs that complement the bluish flowers. It grows 24" (60 cm) in height and 12" (30 cm) in width.

Harvesting and Processing
Borage is best enjoyed throughout the growing season because the plant's nutrients are at their height at this time, and leaves and flowers are almost impossible to preserve or dry for later use. Young and immature leaves should be picked shortly before use. Mature leaves are better suited for use in herbal teas and cold summer soups.

The flowers can be candied for desserts by removing the black anthers, lightly brushing the petals with gently whipped egg whites and

Candied borage flowers

dusting with super-fine sugar. Let them dry before storing. Adding flowers to your ice cube trays will preserve them for cold drinks beyond the growing season.

Borage is not much used in crafts, but has some medicinal uses. It is considered an all-purpose herb and a must-have in the herbalist's kit. It's also beloved by beekeepers and gardeners for its attractiveness to pollinating insects.

Uses
The young leaves add a cucumber flavour to salads and sandwiches. The blossoms can be candied or used fresh, scattered over fruit cups and in cool, refreshing drinks, including iced tea and lemonade. The leaves add a light and subtle flavour to chicken and fish dishes.

Calamint

Calamintha

Calamints are fragrant, aromatic and tasty perennials that deserve a bigger place in our gardens and pantries. Cooks may be familiar with lesser calamint, *C. nepeta*, or common calamint, *C. sylvatica*, which is a little less pungent but used in the same way. Related to savory, calamints are very versatile and useful in a number of dishes. The entire plant is reminiscent of mint with notes of thyme and camphor. It is warm and refreshing in the mouth, peppery with a light bitterness. It is easy to grow and is adorable in the landscape, producing softly fuzzy leaves and tubular flowers in spring colours whose shape resembles pouting lips.

Features
Parts used: whole plant, leaves
Hardiness: zones 5–10

Growing
Calamint prefers to grow in a location with **full sun**. It can tolerate partial shade. The soil should be **alkaline, well drained** and **of average fertility**. It can be propagated by division or grown from seed.

Tips
A herb garden is an ideal location for this plant because of its practical uses, but calamint also a beautiful plant that is worthy of a place in a perennial border. It should be planted in groups for a bigger impact. Calamint can be grown in containers but only outdoors.

Recommended

C. grandiflora (calamint, large-flowered calamint, showy savory) is a hardy perennial that produces square stems that arise from creeping rootstock. Flower spikes with lilac-pink flowers swirl around the tall stems that rise up to 24" (60 cm) in height. Mint-scented, toothed, oval leaves are produced sparingly along those stems. This species spreads 12" (30 cm). **'Variegata'** produces cream variegated leaves.

C. nepeta (lesser calamint, nepitella, mountain balm) is a perennial that produces small, bicoloured purple and white flowers on stems covered with pale grey, downy leaves.

C. sylvatica (common calamint) is a hardy plant with hairy, mint-scented, toothed leaves and pale lilac flowers with darker spots. It grows up to 24" (60 cm) tall.

Dried calamint

Harvesting and Processing
The leaves can be harvested at any time regardless of flowering. If drying, harvest the leaves and spread them out onto screens or hang by the stems in bunches on drying racks. Once dried, they should be stored in an airtight container.

Uses
Fresh leaves are best for cooking while dried leaves are better for teas. The fresh, young leaves of lesser calamint can be sprinkled into salads and tea for a refreshing boost. Calamint complements the flavour of roasts, stews, game and fish; is wonderful with lentils, beans, eggplant and potatoes; and works well in sauces and marinades for meat and fish. Lesser calamint is commonly used in Sicily, Sardinia and Tuscany to flavour vegetables and mushrooms. In Turkish cuisine, calamint is used as a mild form of mint. It blends well with other herbs, including bay, garlic, oregano, parsley, pepper, thyme, sage and mint.

Calendula

Calendula

Calendula is the perfect annual. It is a relatively low-maintenance plant; it produces abundant seeds that can be shared with friends; its flowers look lovely cut for arrangements; and its seedlings sprout every year in places that need a bit of sunshine. This plant is so useful, I can't imagine a garden without it. For butterflies, it produces a seemingly endless supply of nectar. For people, the petals add a piquant note to green salads. Herbalists have made many claims for its curative powers, and few side effects have been recorded.

Calendula-infused bath products

Features
Other names: pot marigold, English marigold
Parts used: flowers
Hardiness: grown as an annual

Growing
Calendula does equally well in **full sun or partial shade**. It likes cool weather and can withstand a light frost. The soil should be of **average fertility** and **well drained**. A second sowing in mid-summer gives a good fall display. Deadhead to prolong blooming and keep plants looking neat.

Tips
These informal plants are attractive in borders and mixed into the vegetable patch. They can also be used in mixed planters. These cold-hardy annuals often continue flowering until the ground freezes completely.

Recommended
C. officinalis is a vigourous, tough, upright plant; it bears single or double, daisy-like flowers in a range of yellow and orange shades. This plant grows 12–24" (30–60 cm) tall, with a slightly lesser spread. **'Bon Bon'** is a dwarf plant that grows 10–12" (25–30 cm) tall and comes in all colours. **'Fiesta Gitana'** ('Gypsy Festival') is a dwarf plant with flowers in a wide range of colours. **'Pacific Beauty'** is a larger plant, growing about 18" (46 cm) tall. It bears large flowers in varied colours.

Harvesting and Processing
The petals and whole flowers can be picked throughout the blooming cycle. They can be used fresh or dried, as well as in infused oil preparations for later use. Simply steep petals in warm vegetable oil; however, the resulting infusion will only last for a few of weeks

Calendula mixed with dill and poppies (above), nasturtiums and calendula (below)

when kept at room temperature. The petals can also be frozen into ice cubes for cool drinks or cooking once the blooming cycle is complete.

Uses

Also known as "poor man's saffron," calendula flowers are popular kitchen herbs that can be added to stews for colour and flavour. The petals also add lively colour to pasta, rice, potatoes, cakes and muffins. Eaten fresh, the petals have a slightly bitter flavour, but they mellow after cooking. Tossed into salads, fresh petals offer nutrition in the form of lutein, a powerful antioxidant. Combined with mint or lemon-flavoured herbs, calendula petals are a pleasant addition to herbal teas.

Calendula flowers are appreciated equally for cosmetic, craft and cooking purposes. Anti-inflammatory, antiseptic, antibacterial and

C. officinalis 'Apricot Sunrise' (above), calendula and bachelor's buttons (below)

antifungal properties are all present in those bright little petals. Because of these attributes, the petals are often used in ointments for soothing irritated and chapped skin, eczema, insect bites and sunburns. They are also used in handmade creams and soaps for the face and hands.

Medicinally, it can be brewed into an infusion that can be used topically to wash minor cuts and bruises.

The name calendula comes from the Latin kalendae, *which translates to "first day of the month," in the Roman calendar, because they tend to flower at the beginning of most months of the year.*

Caraway

Carum

Caraway is one of those herbs that isn't always considered when planting a herb garden, but it has many uses and deserves to become a Canadian landscape staple. Little of this plant is wasted because most of it can be used for a variety of tasty treats. Many cultures use caraway in such foods as cookies, breads, cakes, stewed fruit, cabbage and meat dishes as well as to flavour cheeses and garnish salads. It also flavours a liqueur called Kümmel. The possibilities for caraway may not be endless, but having it in your garden or in a pot on your windowsill will open up new taste sensations in your daily cooking.

Caraway seeds

Features
Parts used: leaves, seeds, root, essential oil from the seeds
Hardiness: zones 3–9, biennial

Growing
Caraway prefers to grow in **full sun**. The soil should be **deep, fertile** and **well drained**. Caraway will tolerate heavier soils. Because of its biennial nature, seed is borne in the second summer. Caraway does not transplant well because of its taproot. It's best to directly sow seed into the location where it will spend its life.

Tips
Caraway is a finely detailed, delicate plant, bearing umbels of white flowers. Its graceful appearance complements bolder-leaved plants in mixed beds and borders. Caraway can also be grown in containers, only as long as the depth will accommodate the taproot over time. It is also ideal for herb gardens, when planted in large groupings for impact and a worthwhile harvest.

Recommended
C. carvi is a 24" (60 cm) tall biennial that produces very feathery or fern-like foliage. Clusters of white flowers tower above the foliage, and appear only in the plant's second year of growth. Ridged fruits or seeds follow after the flowers.

Harvesting and Processing
The feathery leaves can be used fresh in salads, stews and vegetable stir-fries. The seeds are the most commonly used part of the plant and should be harvested from the plant before they have a chance

to fall to the ground. The seeds ripen roughly one month after the flowers are finished. Once the seeds turn brown, they can be harvested by cutting the seedheads from the stems, carefully placing them into a brown paper bag allowing the seeds to freely fall when completely ripe. Keep the bag in a dry, warm location with adequate air circulation.

The roots can be dug up after the second season, and after the foliage and flowerheads have been harvested. If you have room in your garden, sow a second crop of caraway strictly for the root because it's best when young and tender. Caraway root can be peeled and cooked liked a parsnip.

Uses

Many people have probably had a piece of rye bread with caraway seeds at one time or another, but that's certainly

Flowering caraway (all photos)

not where the use of this plant ends. Dishes made with such vegetables as cauliflower, carrots and parsnips are the ideal base for caraway. Popular in German and Austrian cuisine, caraway seeds are thought to diminish the odour caused from cooking cabbage, not to mention add a subtle new flavour to this leafy side dish. Young leaves can be added to soups, salads and sandwiches for a mild, dill-like flavour.

The flavour released from the seeds can change during cooking, so it's best to add the seeds during the last 10 to 15 minutes of cooking or baking.

Caraway seeds have been used medicinally to help settle an upset stomach. Crush and steep a tiny amount in boiling water or warm milk. Crushing releases the beneficial compounds.

Catnip

Nepeta

Cat lovers are more than aware of the positive attributes of catnip, but gardeners may not be as familiar with the uses more appropriate to humans. In the garden, catnip has been found to be a natural insect repellent against aphids, Colorado potato beetles and squash bugs, making this plant perfect for the organic gardener. Its uses don't end there, however, as catnip has so much more to offer beyond the entertainment value of watching your cats roll around on the floor.

Flowering catnip wreath

Features

Other names: dog mint, nep-in-a-hedge
Parts used: leaves, flowers and stems
Hardiness: zones 3–7

Growing

Catnip plants grow well in **full sun** or **partial shade**. Soil should be of **average fertility** and **well drained**. Plants will tend to flop over in rich soil. Pinch tips throughout the growing season to delay flowering and make the plants more compact. Once the plants are almost finished blooming, you may cut them back by one-third to one-half. This will encourage new growth and might prompt them to bloom again in late summer or fall. Divide in spring or fall when the plants begin to look overgrown and dense.

Tips

Catnip plants can be used to edge borders and pathways and can be mixed into herb gardens and with roses. Catnip is also great for containers, both big and small, either by itself or mixed with other plants.

Recommended

N. cataria is a hardy perennial that produces aromatic, coarsely textured foliage with scalloped edges. This erect and bushy plant bears spike-like flowers in light shades of pink and purple in the summer months. The species will grow approximately 36" (90 cm) tall and 12–18" (30–46 cm) wide. **'Citriodora'** is a lemon-scented cultivar that is available but may be difficult to find. It is well worth the search, however.

Harvesting and Processing

Pinching the tips or newest growth from the stems throughout the growing season is best. This will encourage the plant to branch out and remain dense. In regions with a fall killing frost, cut the stems to the ground just before hard frost and hang in bunches in a warm area with adequate air circulation. The dried leaves, flowers and stems can be used for months after they've thoroughly dried.

Catnip is not prone to pests. However, the roots and crown can suffer from rot during cold and wet winters.

Flowering catnip with celeriac, thyme, rosemary, peppers and dandelion (above left), dried catnip leaves and flowers (below left), catnip, greenleaf lettuce, Vietnamese coriander (below)

Uses

Catnip has long been cultivated for its reputed medicinal and culinary qualities. The leaves can be steeped in boiling water for use as a stimulating, minty tea. It is said that catnip tea reduces nervous tension and anxiety, induces sleep and can lower a fever. Regardless of the effect it may have, the magnesium and manganese it contains are sure to be a health benefit. Fresh leaves can be chopped up for soups, sauces, stews, pasta and vegetable dishes. The youngest tips can be minced and sprinkled on salads for extra flavour.

Crafters can use the dried bunches in potpourri and arrangements, in areas where the aroma can be most enjoyed. Leafy catnip stems can also be intertwined with the stems of lemon balm, lemon verbena, marjoram, a variety of mints and scented geraniums into small wreaths or herbal garland to hang in your closets and pantries.

It is no mystery where this plant gets its name—cats love it! Dried leaves stuffed into cloth toys will amuse kittens for hours.

Flowering catnip in raised bed

Chamomile

Chamaemelum

You too can grow your own crop of medicinal chamomile, just in time for those moments when you need to slow things down and calm your frazzled nerves. This delicate-looking plant is also frequently used in a variety of toiletries and bath products and although the culinary uses are few, they are fun.

Features

Other names: Roman chamomile, German chamomile
Parts used: flowers
Hardiness: zones 5–9

Growing

Chamomile prefers locations with **full sun to light shade**. **Well-drained, moist** and **light** soil is best. Starting with young plants is best, but you can also try sowing seed into small peat pots for transplanting later on. Transplanting offsets and division are also means of propagating chamomile.

Tips

This aromatic herb is perfectly suited to herb gardens. It is also an attractive plant and mixes well in borders, but it can become invasive. It's often used as a groundcover between stepping stones in pathways and is well suited to cottage garden settings and containers.

Recommended

C. nobile is a mat-forming perennial that grows 3–12" (8–30 cm) tall and 12" (30 cm) wide. It produces aromatic, divided, delicate, thread-like foliage on a stalkless form. The scent is reminiscent of apples. In summer, daisy-like flowers are produced on tall stems. **'Flore Pleno'** has double, button-like flowers, growing 6" (15 cm) tall and 18" (96 cm) wide. **'Treneague'** is a strongly scented, non-flowering cultivar. This low-growing selection is dense and bushy and less vigorous than the species. Its stems will root wherever they come in contact with the soil.

Harvesting and Processing

Harvest the flowers when they are fully open. Spread the flowers on a

Chamomile facial bath

screen or sheet of paper until dry and store in a dark, airtight container. Once dried, the flowers can be used for a variety of purposes.

Uses

Chamomile is used to make a tea that's often used as a sedative, as well as an aid to digestion after meals. It's also very tasty in fruit dishes, in salads and to flavour cream or light cheeses. This herb has also been used in cosmetics and crafts for generations, as an ingredient in facial oils, floral water and compresses. Crafters use the flowers in potpourri, dried arrangements, garlands and in sachets for scenting closets and drawers. Create a facial mask by combining the flowers with bran, honey and boiling water, or a hair conditioner by mixing chamomile and a handful of scented geranium leaves into hot water. Once cooled, both concoctions are a refreshing treat for your skin and hair. Throw a sachet filled with chamomile into the bath for a soothing soak.

Chenopodium

Chenopodium

Good King Henry, fat hen, American wormseed, epazote, lamb's quarters, goosefoot, ambrosia and huizontle are names that may sound more familiar than the genus or botanical name *Chenopodium*, but there are too many great species to list just one. With each species comes different uses, some of which are noted here. Mostly chenopodium is used in the kitchen and is definitely worth experimenting with because it offers a variety of health benefits and kicks things up a notch in your cooking. Herbs from this unique and versatile genus are staples in the diets of some cultures and are considered to be more vegetable than herb.

Features
Other names: goosefoot
Parts used: leaves, flower spikes
Hardiness: zones 3–9 and annual

Growing

All species of chenopodium prefer a location in **full sun**. The soil should be **well-drained, light** and **rich with organic matter**. Hardy species that have spent a year or more in a container should be divided and repotted annually in spring and amended with new compost.

Tips

Chenopodium species are attractive in the middle to the back of borders, and have more impact mass planted. They can also be integrated into herb and vegetable gardens or grown in containers on a deck or balcony.

Recommended

C. album (fat hen, lamb's quarters, white goosefoot, common pigweed, all good, muckweed) is a tall annual that produces small, greenish white flowers and arrowhead-shaped leaves.

C. bonus-henricus (good King Henry) produces small clusters of green-yellow flowers and triangular or arrowhead-shaped, deep green foliage with a coarse texture. The flowers are borne in tall flower spikes.

Harvesting and Processing

Chenopodium needs at least one year to develop before harvesting. Those living in colder zones should grow the hardier species rather than the annual, to allow time for the plant to develop. After a year's growth, young shoots 6" (15 cm) long can be harvested in mid-spring, and eaten like asparagus. Harvest flowering spikes as they begin to open. Collect the larger leaves later in the season and use as a spinach

Steamed chenopodium

substitute. Use leaves only when fresh or fresh-frozen, and use frozen leaves only in cooked dishes. To freeze, finely chop the leaves and mix with enough water to freeze in an ice cube tray.

Uses

The leaves are rich in vitamin B1, C, calcium and iron and are helpful to those who suffer from anemia. Crushing the leaves also results in a useful dye. The flower spikes can be eaten like broccoli; the young leaves are similar to spinach and can be used raw in salads or cooked into casseroles, stuffings, purées, soups and spicy pies. The shoots can be blanched in hot water, followed by a quick dip in cold water to stop the cooking process, and used in a variety of dishes. Peel only if necessary and serve with a variety of vinaigrette dressings as a change from asparagus.

The seed of *C. album* can be ground into a flour and used to make a thin version of oatmeal or hot cereal.

Chervil

Anthriscus

Chervil has earned its rightful place in the kitchen. It's been used for centuries for various culinary purposes and by homeopaths for medicinal purposes, but it's also grown by gardeners for its delicate beauty.

Features
Other names: French parsley
Parts used: leaves
Hardiness: annual

Growing

Chervil grows well in **partial shade**, in any **well-drained, moist** soil. Sow seed directly into the soil, whether in the ground or in a container, because the seedlings are too delicate to transplant. This frost-tender herb should only be sown after the risk of frost has passed.

Chervil can go to seed very quickly in locations with hot summers. To prevent this from occurring, pinch the flowers out as they begin to emerge and allow the plant to divert its energy into dense, leafy growth.

Tips

Chervil can be grown in a herbal garden, whether for culinary or medicinal purposes, but it also works well in an ornamental setting. The delicate, divided leaves are the perfect foil for bold-leaved plants such as cannas, colocasia and hostas.

Recommended

A. cerefolium is an erect-growing annual with scented, deeply divided foliage that appears almost ferny in nature. The flavour and scent of the foliage is a cross between parsley and anise. The white flower clusters emerge on tall stems in summer. It grows 12–24" (30–60 cm) tall and 12" (30 cm) wide. *A. cerefolium crispum* (curly-leaved chervil) is similar to the species with a less palatable flavour.

Harvesting and Processing

The leaves can be harvested six to eight weeks after planting and throughout the season. The most flavourful leaves are the youngest produced prior to flowering. Continue to pinch the flowers off before

Chervil is often used in *fines herbes*.

they open while harvesting the leaves for use. The leaves can be dried, but they tend to lose some of their flavour in this form.

Uses

Chervil traditionally has been used as one of the four fragrant herbs that make up the bouquet called *fines herbes* in French cuisine. In this bouquet, chervil is combined with chives, tarragon and parsley in equal parts, and all are finely chopped. Chervil has a delicate, parsley-like flavour and is sometimes used in its place. Its uses are very similar to parsley, whether as a garnish or added to salads, soups, sauces, vegetables and meat dishes at the end of cooking. Chervil's light flavour combines well with eggs, poultry and soft cheeses. Best used fresh, the leaves can be preserved frozen in ice-cube trays for use all year long.

Medicinally, chervil leaves can be steeped to create an infusion that stimulates digestion and relieves head colds.

Chervil and radishes are fine companions in the garden, resulting in hotter radishes.

Chicory

Cichorium

Chicory has been an important herb and vegetable for thousands of years. Its properties range from medicinal to culinary, and it was once relied upon as a "floral clock" because of the regular opening and closing of its flowers, which open to the sun and close roughly five hours later. Roasted, ground chicory roots have been used to make a coffee-like drink since the 17th century. Charles Dickens even recommended this beverage in his magazine *House-hold Words*, more than 200 years after it was first used for that purpose. Once you discover the many ways that you can used this herb, you'll find yourself adding it to your herb garden for something a little different.

Radicchio, also known as Italian chicory

Features

Other names: endive, succory, wild chicory
Parts used: leaves, roots
Hardiness: zones 4–8

Growing

Chicory prefers to grow in **full sun**. The soil should be **well drained** and **fertile**. Seed can be sown in the garden directly or into containers in early spring. Seedlings can be planted out once the risk of frost has passed unless they've been hardened off, in which case, they can be planted sooner.

Tips

Chicory, like any herb, is always a fine addition to a herb garden, but the pretty violet-blue flowers are attractive enough to mix into a flowerbed to add to the summer's profusion of blooms. It is a little too large for containers, however, unless you can provide some type of support, such as an obelisk.

Recommended

C. intybus is a clump-forming perennial that grows up to 4' (1.2 m) tall and 24" (60 cm) wide. Toothed, tongue-shaped leaves are produced along with bluish purple, cornflower-like flowers. Occasionally white or pink flowers are produced as well. This plant has a substantial taproot.

There are different types or phases of chicory, depending on what you're growing the plant for. The following types are grown for their leaves, which grow in both a head form similar to lettuce and on the stems above the basal leaves, prior to flowering.

Non-forcing chicory selections are available including **'Crystal Head,' 'Sugar Loaf'** (Pain de Sucre) and **'Snowflake.'** The leaves of non-forcing selections do not require blanching. Blanching refers to types that are grown without light, resulting in "bleached" leaves. **'Red Verona,' 'Rosso di Chioggia'** and **'Rosso di Treviso'**

C. intybus (above), *C. intybus* in bloom (opposite page, below)

offer reddish coloured leaves and are great additions to salads. **'Witloof'** (Brussels chicory) is grown for its chicons, or small pastel yellow heads, and requires blanching to preserve its mild flavour.

'Magdeburg' or **'Brunswick'** are the best selections for producing roots which can be used as a coffee substitute.

Harvesting and Processing

The newest leaves, harvested from the stems, can be picked throughout the growing season. The older leaves tend to be quite bitter. The leaves can be eaten fresh but also dried. For drying, pick unblemished, young leaves and spread them out on a wire rack in a cool, dark place with adequate air circulation. Once dry, place the leaves into an airtight container. Whole,

washed leaves can be frozen in foil for weeks or chopped and mixed with a little water in ice cube trays.

Types that are grown for their heads, or chicons, should be harvested when very young, when they are tender and not too bitter. To preserve the light leaf colouration, grow these selections without light, by either mounding soil over top or by placing an overturned bucket on top of the plant to shield it from light. Another method for blanching is to dig out the number of roots you require for heads in the fall. Remove the foliage and replant the roots tightly together and upright, in a deep box or pot with a sandy soil piled 6" (15 cm) above the top of the roots. Keep the roots in a moist, dark and heated location, such as a greenhouse or warm shed for large quantities, or in your house for a pot or two. It's important for the area to remain very dark; otherwise, the leaves growing underneath the soil may begin to turn green and bitter. As soon as the white leaves begin to show above the soil, the plants are ready for lifting. Once lifted, the blanched, leafy head can be separated from the root.

The leaves used for tea are harvested from the taller stems or stalks that form if the plant is allowed to grow beyond the "lettuce" stage. The leaves can be used fresh or dried.

The roots can be harvested at any point. In order to use the roots as a coffee substitute, they have to be roasted. To roast chicory, chop fresh roots, place in a single layer on a cookie sheet and roast in a 325° F (160° C) oven for about 30 minutes, stirring every 10 minutes. Roasted chicory roots can easily be made into a tea—just grind them in a coffee grinder and steep.

Uses

Either on its own or combined with other herbs, chicory root makes a fine substitute for coffee. Simply combine 2 tsp (10 mL) dried, chopped burdock root, 1 tsp (5 mL) each roasted chicory root and dried, chopped dandelion root, ½ oz (14 g) licorice root and 1 qt (1 L) water. Combine herbs and water, simmer on low heat 20 to 30 minutes, strain herbs and serve. Sweetener and/or milk can be added if desired. The stem leaves can be used for medicinal purposes, such as in a tea for digestive upset, among other ailments.

Ground chicory root

When chicory is grown for the heads, it's often used more as a vegetable than a herb. It can be eaten raw in salads and sandwiches. The leaves can be boiled and added to cheese sauces or simply served as a side vegetable.

Chives

Allium

Chives have been in people's gardens for over 5000 years, and today this herb knows no geographical limit. The delicate onion flavour of chives is the mildest in the onion family. Chives are also one of the easiest herbs to grow and most commonly used in the kitchen. In whatever culinary creation you concoct in which onions are present, you can substitute chives for a slightly different, milder flavour. The best place to start is by snipping some chives onto a steamy baked potato, smothered in sour cream.

Chives planted in a flowerbed

Features

Other names: fine chives
Parts used: leaves, flowers
Hardiness: zones 3–8

Growing

Chives grow best in **full sun**. The soil should be **fertile, moist** and **well drained**, but chives adapt to most soil conditions. These plants are easy to start from seed, but they do like the soil temperature to stay above 65° F (19° C) before they will germinate, so seeds started directly in the garden are unlikely to sprout before early summer. To keep the plants vigorous and healthy, dig up and divide the clumps every couple of years, once the flowers have faded in late summer. If you are not growing chives for the flowers, then cut the plant to the ground two or three times during the growing season to promote fresh growth from the base.

Tips

Chives are decorative enough to be included in a mixed or herbaceous border and can be left to naturalize. In an herb garden, chives should be given plenty of space to allow self-seeding. Chives can also be grown in containers, allowing you to bring them in for the winter months.

Recommended

A. schoenoprasum (chives) forms a clump of bright green, cylindrical leaves. Clusters of pinky purple flowers are produced in early and mid-summer. It grows 12–24" (30–60 cm) tall and 12" (30 cm) wide. **'Forescate'** produces pink-purple flowers. **'Grolau'** was developed for indoor use, has thicker leaves and a stronger flavour and produces best when cut frequently. **'Ruby Gem'** has ornamental grey foliage and red flowers.

Chive butter (above), chives with oregano, thyme and sage (below)

'**Staro**' is a hybrid with thicker leaves ideal for freezing.

A. tuberosum (garlic chives, Chinese chives, Chinese leeks) is a fast-growing species that is very similar to the above species in appearance, but the leaves taste more like a combination of chives and garlic, and are more flat than round. The flowers are white.

Harvesting and Processing

Chives should be used fresh. Dried chives are available but lack flavour. Ideally, snipping chives from the plant is the easiest, most convenient method of harvest during the outdoor growing season. If you've chosen to grow chives indoors as well, then removing a leaf or two for cooking will not only enhance your meals, but will also encourage the plant to remain dense and full. If you can't grow it indoors, harvest the fresh leaves toward the end of the season before the frost, mince and freeze with a enough water to fill an ice cube tray. The flowers are best when fresh.

Uses

Mix chives into dips or sprinkle them on salads and baked potatoes. Chives also work well in herb butters, or when flavouring cream cheese or other mild, spreadable cheeses. Cheese and cream sauces can be mildly complemented by chives without being overwhelmed by them.

The flowers are perfect for herbal vinegar, because they not only enhance the flavour of the vinegar, but also give it a rosy pink hue. The flowers can be used as an edible garnish. Gently break them up and use them in combination with the leaves, or on their own.

A. schoenoprasum (above), chive vinegar (below)

Chives are said to increase appetite and encourage good digestion. They are also very high in vitamins C and A and calcium, and possess antibacterial and antifungal properties.

Chives are companion plants to carrots. When the two are grown in close proximity, carrots tend to grow larger.

Coriander · Cilantro

Coriandrum

Both coriander and cilantro use dates back to biblical times. Today they're commonly used in a variety of ethnic cuisine including Mexican, Mediterranean, Cajun and Asian. Coriander is a multi-purpose herb. The leaves, called cilantro and used in salads, salsas and soups, and the seeds, called coriander and used in pies, chutneys and marmalades, have distinct flavours and culinary uses. The seeds are used in breads and cakes, not only for their flavour, but also because of the digestive action the seeds have on breaking down carbohydrates.

Features

Other names: Chinese parsley
Parts used: leaves, seeds
Hardiness: tender annual

Growing

Coriander prefers **full sun**, but tolerates partial shade. The soil should be **fertile, light** and **well drained**. These plants dislike humid conditions and do best during a dry summer. Preventing the plant from flowering will produce the best leaf development. Deadhead regularly unless you plan on using the flowers.

Tips

Coriander has pungent leaves and is best planted where people will not have to brush past it. It is, however, a delight to behold when in flower. Add a plant or two here and there throughout your borders and vegetable garden, both for the visual appeal and to attract beneficial insects.

Recommended

C. sativum forms a clump of lacy basal foliage above which large, loose clusters of tiny, white flowers are produced. The seeds ripen in late summer and fall. It grows up to 24" (60 cm) tall and 12–18" (30–46 cm) wide. **'Cilantro'** produces very flavourful foliage. **'Morocco'** is a fine selection for seed production.

Harvesting and Processing

Harvesting the leaves throughout the growing season is highly recommended because they are most flavourful when used fresh. Choose the lower or older leaves for the strongest flavour unless you desire a milder flavour. The stems can also be eaten when young and tender.

Coriander flowers and seeds

Coriander should be stored stem down in water and covered with a plastic bag. The leaves can be frozen in ice-cube trays for use year-round. The flowers are also flavourful and reminiscent of the leaves, but are sweeter; pick them as they open. Collect the seeds as soon as they ripen. A sure sign that they are ripe is when they turn brown and harden later in the season. If you're growing the plants strictly for the seed, leave the flowers intact and try not to remove too much of the foliage because the plant will need as much energy to get to the seed stage as possible. The seeds should be dry before use and stored in an airtight container.

Uses

The leaves can be used in soups, stews, spring rolls, salads, salsas and many other dishes. To preserve their flavour, add the leaves toward the end of the cooking time. The seeds can be used in cakes and cookies, as well as curries, chutneys and pickles. The flowers can be used as a substitute for the leaves when a sweeter flavour is called for.

Cress

Lepidium

Cress is not one plant but a group of botanically unrelated plants grown for their sharp, peppery or mustard-like flavour. Upland cress, *Barbarea verna*, and broadleaf or curly cress, *Lepidium sativum*, are easier to grow than watercress, *Nasturtium officinale*, which requires very moist soil at all times. Most people know cress for its use in dainty, crustless finger sandwiches. As yummy as finger sandwiches are, there are far better ways to use cress. For our purposes, we're going to focus on just one of the species, *L. sativum*, because of its strong peppery flavour and ease of growth.

Features
Other names: garden cress, pepperweed, land cress
Parts used: leaves
Hardiness: tender annual

Growing

Cress thrives in **full sun to light shade** in soil that is **very moist**, **well drained** and of **average fertility**. Sow seed directly in early spring or late summer through fall, or grow it on a windowsill and harvest the sprouts. Continuous crops will provide you with fresh cress all growing season. Sow in all but the hottest months to prevent the plants from bolting or going to seed before making enough leaf growth to harvest.

Tips

Cress is suitable for the herb garden, but leave enough space for a succession of crops throughout the growing season. Cress can also be grown in containers, making it ideal for growing indoors year-round. When grown for sprouts, cress can be grown or sprouted on wet paper towels between two layers of plastic or in a plastic container.

Recommended

L. sativum is a reseeding annual that produces deeply cut, lacy leaves on single, erect stems. Small, almost spherical flowers are produced only three to four weeks after sowing. It grows 6" (15 cm) tall and wide.
'Bubbles' produces leaves with ruffled edges and blistered surfaces that are quite hot to taste. This cultivar is also slower to bolt than others.
'Greek' produces flat, dissected leaves that are spicy, sweet and nutty in flavour.

All cresses are abundant in vitamins and minerals, containing iron, iodine, phosphorus and sulfur, all of which the body needs.

Chicken and cress sandwich

Harvesting and Processing

Always use cress fresh. To harvest, cut back plants halfway, and they will resprout before flowering. When grown indoors purely for use as sprouts (immature plants), use sprouting trays just as you would for other vegetables and herbs. The sprouting trays don't require any soil to grow and allow you to harvest the sprouts all year long. If you can only grow it outdoors but would like to use it year-round, mince it, mix with water in ice cube trays and freeze for later use.

Uses

Cress is invaluable in salads and sandwiches and as a garnish for its spicy flavour and finely curled, nutritious leaves. Cress perfectly complements egg dishes, including omelettes and quiches. Cress soup has an unusual and unique flavour. Cress can also be used as a substitute for spinach in dishes where a stronger flavour is required. Most meat dishes will benefit from a little cress added at the end of cooking.

Curry

Helichrysum

This plant can be a little confusing to some people because curry is not the result of one plant. It is commonly known as curry simply because the flavour of the leaves is reminiscent of curry powder, which is a combination of many spices including cumin, coriander, cayenne, cloves, cardamom, turmeric and mustard seed among others. Curry is also a pretty little ornamental. Its silvery grey colour will stand out in a mixed perennial border as well as decorative containers filled with annuals and herbs, offering colour, aroma and functionality.

Potpourri with dried curry leaves

Features

Other names: curry plant
Parts used: leaves, flowers
Hardiness: zones 7–10, grown as an annual in most zones

Growing

This plant prefers to grow in **full sun** but will tolerate partial shade. The soil should be **well drained** and **poor to moderately fertile**.

Tips

The contrasting colours of curry complement just about any container, whether it's a mix of shades or monochromatic. The silver foliage lends itself well to areas in the garden that need a little brightening, and the yellow flowers are sure to grab people's attention. Herb gardens are, of course, a common destination for this plant as well.

When prepared as an essential oil, curry is used to augment the flavour of fruit-flavoured treats and fragrances.

Recommended

H. italicum is a tender perennial that grows up to 18" (46 cm) in height and 24" (60 cm) in spread. It is a dense plant bearing silvery grey, needle-like leaves and clusters of yellow flowers that stand tall above the foliage.

Harvesting and Processing

The leaves and flowers can be used fresh throughout the growing season, but they are also useful when dried. After pinching off the leaves and flowers, either during the growing season or just before frost for the last harvest of the season, place them into a paper bag to dry, in a cool, dark and dry location.

Uses

Sprigs of *H. italicum* can be added to rice and vegetable dishes for a hint of curry flavour.

The dried leaves and flowers can also be added to potpourris and sachets, not only for their spicy fragrance but also for their insecticidal properties, ideal in closets and wardrobes.

Dandelion

Taraxacum

Ok, ok, I know what you're thinking. Dandelion? How could I possibly use a weed that's taking over my front yard? Well the time has come to embrace the dandelion. Believe me, it's much easier than constantly fighting it, and eventually you'll find yourself touting the benefits of dandelion to all of your friends. Dandelion has been used medicinally for thousands of years. It's also been a staple among certain cuisines for almost as long. Every part of the plant can be used, and clearly it's easy to grow. All you have to do is get past what we've always been led to believe. Dandelion is a useful plant, attractive even, and offers more in the way of uses than some commonly known vegetables. If you're willing to try one new thing this year, make it dandelion.

Dried dandelion root

Features

Parts used: leaves, flowers, root
Hardiness: zones 3–10

Growing

Dandelions prefer to grow in **full sun** but will grow in just about any lighting situation. The soil should be **well drained**. Add liberal amounts of compost to areas you're sowing if you plan on harvesting the roots. Dandelion readily reseeds itself, but often in places where you'd rather it didn't grow.

Tips

Dandelions can be added to your herb garden or they can be grown in a block or row in your vegetable garden. Dandelions can also be directly sown into containers for harvest closer to the kitchen.

Recommended

T. officinale is a hardy perennial that grows up to 12" (30 cm) tall. It produces long, deeply toothed leaves and deep yellow flowers on tall, hollow stems. The brightly coloured flowers quickly change from yellow to fluffy, airy seedheads that are easily taken by the first summer breeze. Dandelions over time develop a deep and some-what extensive root system, almost tap-root-like. **'Thick-leaved Improved'** produces a tender, thicker leaf with less bitterness. **'Verte de Montgomery'** is very similar to the wild varieties in your yard, which are ripe for the picking and just as tasty.

Dandelion flowers

Harvesting and Processing

A few weeks before harvesting the leaves, cover the plants with a dark, opaque fabric to block out most of the light to blanch the leaves and reduce their bitterness. The youngest leaves are the least bitter and most flavourful. The tender leaves can be picked throughout the growing season. The

Dandelion leaves are high in vitamins A and C and contain high levels of potassium, phosphorus, calcium, iron, copper and magnesium.

flowers should be picked when bright, yellow and young. Use the flowers fresh, making sure to remove all of the stem. To prevent the flowers from closing after cutting, place them into a bowl of cold water and take them out just before eating or serving them.

The roots can be harvested at any time. Chop the dried roots into 2" (5 cm) pieces and roast at 300° F (150° C) for about 10 minutes. Grind the roasted pieces, adding a quarter teaspoon to your coffee or hot chocolate for a new flavour.

Do not eat dandelions that have been in contact with lawn fertilizers, herbicides or any other synthetic chemical contaminants.

Uses

The leaves are delicious in salads and are a fine substitute for spinach. The flavour of bacon is the perfect complement to dandelion leaves; they also work beautifully in fresh vegetable dishes. Many soups and casseroles benefit from the addition of dandelion leaves.

The crowns are a delicacy when deep fried, and the roots can be used as a coffee substitute after being roasted and ground.

The flowers can be fermented into wine, used fresh in salads and fried in butter. The young buds are high in protein. Unopened flower buds are tender and tasty, and they add a tasty crunch in green salads.

Dandelion leaves and roots (above), dandelion grown with perennials (below)

Dill

Anethum

Once known for warding off evil spells, dill is not only part of folklore throughout Canada but is also a part of our culinary history. Dill leaves and seeds are probably best known for their use as pickling herbs, though they have a wide variety of other culinary uses. The perfect example of a dish I can't imagine without fresh springs of dill is boiled new potatoes straight out of the garden, smothered in butter and sour cream. Dill is another herb that is incredibly easy to grow, requiring nothing more than a little space. The rest will take care of itself.

Fresh dill stems (top), dried dill leaves (left) and dill seeds (right)

Features
Other names: dillweed
Parts used: leaves, seeds
Hardiness: annual

Growing
Dill grows best in **full sun** in a **sheltered location** out of strong winds. The soil should be of **poor to average fertility, moist** and **well drained**. Sow seeds every couple of weeks in spring and early summer to ensure a regular supply of leaves. Plants should not be grown near fennel because they will cross-pollinate and the seeds will lose their distinct flavours.

Dill turns up frequently in historical records as both a culinary and a medicinal herb. It was used by the Egyptians and Romans and is mentioned in the Bible.

Tips
With its feathery leaves, dill is an attractive addition to a mixed bed or border. It can be included in a vegetable garden, but does well in any sunny location. It also attracts predatory insects to the garden.

Recommended
A. graveolens forms a clump of feathery, finely cut, aromatic foliage. Clusters of yellow flowers are borne at the tops of sturdy stems. It grows 2–5' (60 cm–1.5 m) tall and 12" (30 cm) or more wide. **'Bouquet'** produces high seed and leaf yields. **Var. 'Fernleaf'** produces high yields of leaves in a dwarf form and is slow to bolt. **'Hercules'** is an extremely tall selection with a dense, leafy habit. **'Mammoth'** produces sparse foliage and quickly goes to seed, producing large seed heads. It is one of the best for pickling. **'Vierling'** is the best selection for ornamental use but the leaves are edible, too. It bears steel blue foliage and chartreuse blooms with strong stems and early flowers.

Flowering dill (above and opposite page)

Harvesting and Processing

Fresh dill is by far the best, but when the growing season ends, it's time to remove the foliage from the stems for drying. Dried dill can be as tasty when the leafy stalks are cut before the flowerheads appear. Spread the stalks on a wire rack in a shady, cool location until dry. Gently rub the dried leaves from the stalks into an airtight container. Fresh dill leaves can also be frozen for later use by finely chopping them, mixing them with water and pouring the mixture into an ice cube tray.

The seeds will ripen in the fall and can be collected as soon as they begin to fall from the seedheads. Remove the heads and spread out onto to a tray to sit in the sun for drying. Once dry, gently shake the seeds from the heads into an airtight container.

Uses

Dill not only tastes delicious but it also helps with the digestion of certain foods, including cabbage, bread and cooked root vegetables. Dill is a pleasant complement to most dishes, both cold and hot. Mix a little into your cottage cheese or cream cheese. Egg and potato dishes were made for dill. This herb also works well in salad dressings, sauces and most rice, lamb and fish dishes. Dill has been used in a variety of ethnic cuisine including Scandinavian, Middle Eastern, Mediterranean, Thai, Vietnamese and Laotian.

The seeds have been used in pickling for generations for baby cucumbers, carrots or cabbage.

A popular Scandinavian dish called gravlax is made by marinating a fillet of salmon with oil, salt, sugar and the leaves and seeds of dill.

Dill-flavoured cream cheese (above)

Elderberry

Sambucus

Elderberries have what we all want in a shrub—flowers (often fragrant), berries, interesting foliage and a practical use for almost every part of the plant. Cultivars with varied leaf characteristics and habits are bringing a new level of awareness to this group of plants. On the other hand, most selections need pruning to keep them looking tidy.

Fresh and dried elderberries

Features
Other names: elder
Parts used: flowers, berries
Hardiness: zones 3–9

Growing
Elderberries grow well in **full sun** or **partial shade**. Cultivars with burgundy or black leaves develop the best colour in **full sun**, while cultivars with yellow leaves develop the best colour in light or partial shade. The soil should be of **average fertility, moist** and **well drained**. These plants tolerate dry soil once established.

Though elderberries do not require pruning, they can become scraggly and untidy if ignored. They will tolerate even severe pruning. Plants can be cut back to within a couple of buds off the ground in early spring. This treatment controls the spread of these vigorous growers and encourages the best foliage colour on specimens grown for this purpose.

Plants cut right back to the ground will not flower or produce fruit that season. If you desire flowers and fruit as well as good foliage colour, remove only one-third to one-half of the growth in early spring. Fertilize or apply a layer of compost after pruning to encourage strong new growth.

Tips
Elderberries can be used in shrub or mixed borders, in natural woodland gardens or next to ponds or other water features. Plants with interesting or colourful foliage can be used as specimen plants or to create focal points in the garden.

Elderberry fruit attracts birds to the garden.

S. racemosa, with clusters of red fruit

Recommended

S. canadensis (*S. nigra* subsp. *canadensis;* American elderberry) is a shrub about 12' (6 m) tall, with an equal spread. White, mid-summer flowers are followed by dark purple berries. This species is generally found growing in damp ditches and alongside rivers and streams. **'Aurea'** has yellow foliage and red fruit. **'Goldfinch'** has finely cut, yellow foliage (Zones 4–9).

S. nigra (*S. nigra* subsp. *nigra;* European elderberry, black elderberry) is a large shrub that can grow 15' (4.6 m) tall and wide. The yellowish white to creamy white, early-summer flowers are followed by purple-black fruit. BLACK BEAUTY ('Gerda') has dark foliage that gets blacker as the season progresses, and pink flowers. It grows 8–12' (2.4–3 m) tall, with an equal spread. **'Laciniata'** has deeply dissected leaflets that give the shrub a feathery appearance. It grows up to 10' (3 m) tall and wide. **'Madonna'** has dark green foliage with wide, irregular, yellow margins. **'Pulverulenta'** has unusually dark green and white mottled foliage. It grows slower than other cultivars but reaches 10' (3 m) in height and spread (Zones 4–8).

Harvesting and Processing

The flowers can be picked soon after opening, and the berries once ripe or fully coloured. The flowers should be rinsed with water before eating or preparation to remove all evidence of insects. Be sure to strain out all seeds, which contain toxins, and consume the berries sparingly because the fruit has a laxative effect.

S. racemosa berries (above), *S. canadensis* in flower (below)

Uses

Both the flowers and the fruit can be used to make wine. The berries are also popular for pies and jelly. The raw berries are marginally edible but not palatable and can cause stomach upset, particularly in children. Cooking the berries before eating them is recommended. Try them in place of blueberries in pies, scones or muffins. The berries can also be transformed into jams and jellies. Fresh flowerheads dipped in batter, fried and dusted with sugar are a tasty delicacy called elderflower fritters. Fresh or dried flowers can be added to desserts and sorbets, along with fresh or cooked gooseberries and stewed fruits.

Cosmetically, elder flowers have been used in a variety of toiletries, including a cream said to reduce the evidence of wrinkles by tightening the skin.

Not all elderberries are edible. The two recommended species listed here are safe, but others may not be. The rule of thumb is that red-fruited species are poisonous and black- or blue-fruited species are edible, but only when ripe and cooked.

Fennel

Foeniculum

Fennel has been part of history for thousands of years in one capacity or other. Herbalists have touted the benefits of this plant for its healing capabilities, and cooks have used fennel both as a vegetable and herb in a variety of ways. This plant even possesses cosmetic qualities said to smooth wrinkles and lines from the face as well as refreshing tired eyes. Once you've tried cooking with fennel, you'll find yourself searching for more and more ways to use this wonderfully tasty and aromatic herb.

F. vulgare 'Bronze' in bloom

Features

Other names: common fennel, sweet fennel

Parts used: leaves, bulb or swollen stem base, seeds

Hardiness: zones 4–9

Growing

Fennel grows best in **full sun**. The soil should be **average to fertile, moist** and **well drained**. Avoid planting fennel near dill and coriander, because cross-pollination reduces seed production and makes the seed flavour of each less distinct. Fennel is also a poor garden companion to caraway, tomatoes, kohlrabi and dwarf beans. Fennel easily self-sows.

Tips

Fennel is an attractive addition to a mixed bed or border, and it can be included in a vegetable garden. It also attracts pollinators and predatory insects to the garden. Fennel can be grown in containers, too. If you're only after young, tender leaves then crowd the pot with at least six plants. If you would also like to harvest the stalks, then reduce that number to three. Marigolds and nasturtiums are the perfect companions in containers and equally as useful. Fennel can also be grown in containers indoors but only for the leaves as it's unlikely to produce the seeds or bulb.

Recommended

F. vulgare is a short-lived perennial that forms clumps of loose, feathery foliage. Clusters of small, yellow flowers are borne in late summer. The seeds ripen in fall. This species is primarily grown for its seeds and leaves. It grows 2–6' (60 cm–1.8 m) tall and 12–24" (30–60 cm) wide. **Var.** *azoricum* (Florence fennel, finocchio) is a biennial that forms a large, edible bulb at the stem base. This variety is grown for its stems, leaves and bulb. The licorice flavoured bulb is popular raw in salads, cooked in soups or stews and roasted

F. vulgare (above), F. vulgare 'Bronze' (below)

like other root vegetables. **Var. *dulce*** (sweet fennel) bears green-brown seeds. **'Purpureum'** (*rubrum*, 'Atro-purpureum', var. *dulce* 'Purpureum', bronze fennel) is similar in appearance to the species but has bronzy purple foliage. This cultivar is usually sold as an ornamental, but its parts are entirely edible.

Harvesting and Processing

The leaves and stems can be harvested all season long. They're most flavourful when used fresh, and drying is not recommended. At the end of the season, before hard frost, cut the stems either to the ground or to the bulb. Discard the tough stems and chop the rest, adding a little water to the mix and fill an ice cube tray or two with the mixture for freezing.

The bulb should be used fresh as a vegetable. To harvest, cut plant at soil level in the fall or when it appears large enough for cooking.

To collect the seeds, remove the seedheads before the seeds start to fall off. It's important to dry them properly before storage to prevent them from getting musty.

Uses

Because of the seductive scent and flavour of licorice, fennel is the perfect complement to certain cuisines and dishes, especially fish. All parts can be used in cooking, whether you snip the leaves and stems into dressings, salads or vegetable dishes, sprinkle the seeds into pastries, pasta and sauces, cook the bulb as a root vegetable or grate it into salads. The leaves and seeds are tasty in herbal vinegars and herbed butters.

Fennel tea is the result of steeping fennel seeds in boiling water. Drinking this tea will help to settle an upset stomach, aid digestion and prevent heartburn and constipation.

Steeping a compress in the tea and placing it on the eyelids will ease inflammation or puffy eyes. A strong fennel infusion combined with honey and buttermilk makes a great cleansing lotion for the face; replace the buttermilk with yogurt and you have the perfect revitalizing face mask.

Crafters appreciate the versatility of this herb as well. The essential oil is commonly used in handmade soaps and fragrances.

Tea made with fennel seeds (above), young fennel and tomato plants (below)

Fenugreek

Trigonella

This herb isn't nearly as well known as some others, such as dill, but it's well worth experimenting with. The dried leaves have been used to flavour root vegetable dishes in Middle Eastern cooking for centuries. Fenugreek is frequently used in Indian cuisine to flavour curries. The leaves are also an important ingredient in tandoori marinades, while the seeds are part of specific curry blends, including the distinctive vindaloo. Fenugreek is principally a cleansing, soothing herb whose sprouts have a variety of tasty uses, and are said to have tonic properties.

Features
Parts used: leaves, seeds
Hardiness: annual

Growing
Fenugreek prefers to grow in a location with **full sun**. **Well-drained, moist, fertile** soil is best. The seed can be sown in early spring and will germinate in cold soils.

Tips
This herb is useful and attractive in a herb garden, but it can also adorn a mixed bed or border. It can also be grown in a decorative container as a specimen or mixed with other herbs, perennials and annuals. When planted as a specimen, it can be brought indoors in the fall, where it will be at your fingertips for easy harvest.

Recommended
T. foenum-graecum is an erect annual that grows 18–24" (46–60 cm) in height. It produces deeply lobed leaves reminiscent of clover but more elongated. Pale yellow flowers emerge in mid-summer followed by a curved pod that comes to a point resembling a beak. Each fruit contains up to 20 light brown, fragrant seeds.

Harvesting and Processing
If you're using the leaves to cook with, pick them once they're fairly large. Use fresh leaves because drying is not recommended. Finely chopping some leaves, combining them with a little water in ice cube trays and freezing them is a reliable way to stretch out your supply of fenugreek through the winter months.

If you're growing for the seed, allow the plant to flower and set fruit. Collect the ripened pods after

Fenugreek stems (above), fenugreek seeds (opposite)

the first few seeds begin to fall from them. Remove the pods and spread onto trays in a dry location. When the pods are dry, shake the seeds from their pods and store them in an airtight container.

Uses
High in vitamins, minerals and iron, fenugreek leaves are cooked as a vegetable, especially in Indian cuisine. Eat fenugreek sprouts as a snack, fresh-in-hand, juiced with vegetables, added to sandwiches and salads or mixed with potato salad and other root vegetables. The sprouts can be used as a garnish, added to soups, rice and pasta dishes and stir-fries, just before serving. Do not cook sprouts because they go mushy.

The seeds are frequently used in curry powder blends. They can also be added to pastries, marinades, pickles and chutneys. Roasted seeds can be used as a coffee substitute.

Garlic

Allium

Garlic is not only incredibly aromatic and flavourful but nutritious too. It is high in vitamins A, B and C, copper, manganese, iron, sulfur and calcium. Medicinally, garlic is an important herb for anyone and everyone, based on the typical North American diet. Garlic also has its place in history. Garlic juice was used in World War I to prevent wounds from becoming septic. Classic writers such as Pliny, Horace, Virgil, and later Chaucer and Shakespeare have all recorded its use. It was even known to Homer, and I'm not talking about Mr. Simpson either. The Romans, Greeks and Egyptians all knew of its excellent properties, just as we do today. Maybe the old adage should have been "eating a clove of garlic a day keeps the doctor away."

Mature garlic plants with straw mulch (above), garlic bulbs (opposite)

Features

Parts used: bulb
Hardiness: zones 3–8

Growing

Garlic should be grown in an area with **full to partial sun. Well-drained, light, alkaline** soil is best.

Separate bulbs into cloves. The cloves or bulblets should be planted in early spring as soon as the frost is out of the ground, with skins intact. The cloves are planted with the pointed end up and the root end facing down. The cloves should be planted 2" (5 cm) deep and 6" (15 cm) apart. Elephant garlic can be planted a little farther apart. It's best to use garlic sets from the garden centre for planting. Use only the largest cloves from the bulb. You can also plant the cloves in the fall for harvest the following summer or fall.

Remove the flowers as they emerge to redirect the energy back into the formation of the bulb.

Tips

Garlic really doesn't have much in the way of an ornamental quality for the garden. It could be planted in a narrow border as an architectural element, but often garlic is planted in a vegetable or herb garden with adequate access for harvest. Garlic can be grown in a container if there is a suitably cold location to store it, such as an unheated garage or shed, during the winter. Be sure that the soil is moist before it is left to freeze and check it from time to time throughout the winter so it isn't allowed to dry out. Move the container outdoors in early spring and it will begin to sprout once the days are warm enough. In warmer regions, a container planted with garlic can remain outdoors year-round.

Garlic bulbs (above & below)

Recommended

A. ampeloprasum (elephant garlic) produces giant bulbs with a milder flavour than the standard species.

A. sativum (common garlic) starts as a bulb, or a tight cluster of bulbs. From that cluster, the bulb produces a sprout of growth that emerges at the soil surface as grass-like leaves 12–24" (30–60 cm) tall. A rigid, tall and straw-like flower stalk grows from the centre of the leaves, topped with a rounded cluster of purple-tinted, tiny flowers that form a globular shape.

Roasted garlic spread on toast

Harvesting and Processing

Once half of the foliage has died back in mid-summer, it's time to dig the garlic up carefully with a garden fork. Leaving the bulbs in the ground until all of the foliage dies back will result in shattered bulbs, which are difficult to remove from the soil. Weather permitting, leave the bulbs on the ground for a few days, but only if it's warm and dry.

After they're dug, shake the soil loose from the bulb. Cut the spent leaves two to three inches above the bulb. Allow the bulbs to dry completely before storing and only store in containers that have good air circulation, including garlic pots and wire baskets, or braid the stems to hang in a pantry.

There are more than 600 varieties of garlic available for cultivation, and each one is unique.

Uses

The list of uses for garlic is endless. It can be used fresh, roasted or cooked to add flavour to a variety of dishes, even ice cream. It can be used whole, chopped, minced or sliced. Each clove packs a punch, so a few go a long way.

Garlic is effective for lowering blood sugar levels and cholesterol, aids in curing fungal infections and boosts the immunity, helping to ward off the common cold and flu.

Ginger Root

Zingiber

I'm sure that most people think ginger is a tropical plant that couldn't possibly be grown in Canada, but you can grow it year-round regardless of what zone you live in. This is where container culture becomes a true blessing, allowing people in cold climates to grow plants they couldn't grow ordinarily. In fact, this is a project you can get the kids involved in because, if nothing else, growing ginger is fun and easy, and will reward you with its sweet, spicy flavour and aroma.

Features
Other names: ginger
Parts used: rhizomes or root
Hardiness: annual

Grated ginger root

Growing

When grown outdoors, ginger root should be in the sunniest spot available, preferably **full sun** if possible. Indoors, it should be positioned in the brightest location or grown under a grow light. The potting mixture or potting soil should be a **light mixture with adequate drainage** and **fertility**. Add compost into the mixture to improve its richness.

Select a container that is at least 12" (30 cm) deep. Cut the fresh root into pieces for several plants, or plant the root whole. Set the root just below the surface of the soil mix. Set the pot in a warm and sunny location and water sparingly until growth emerges. Water thoroughly after shoots appear. Mist occasionally or frequently, depending on your region, to increase the humidity. The pot can also be placed onto a pebble tray filled with water or placed in a room with a humidifier. Put the container outdoors in a sunny location after the risk of frost has passed but make sure to bring it back indoors long before fall frost. It will go dormant during the winter months, slowing down until the day length increases in spring. Repot it annually to accommodate its new growth.

To use ginger for cooking, the skin should be scraped or peeled from the fibrous flesh. Once peeled, ginger can be sliced, chopped, mince, pressed or grated, depending on the recipe.

Ginger roots

Tips

Containers are easily displayed on decks, balconies, porches, steps and around the pool. The foliar display will remind you of tropical destinations, perfect for an exotic themed garden design.

Recommended

Z. officinale is a perennial, tropical herb that is grown primarily for its root. It produces bright green, thick stems with long, strap-like foliage and exotic yellow flowers with hints of green. It can reach 3–4' (90 cm–1.2 m) heights but may take years to get there.

Ginger root is also known as adrak, gin, khing, jeung and shoga in other cultures around the world.

Harvesting and Processing

A year after planting, once the plant is well established, the roots can be dug up. The newer more tender roots that have developed over the year are far more flavourful than the older ones. Cut the stems from the roots, and store in the refrigerator for up to three weeks or more. The roots can also be dried and ground into ginger powder, and stored in an airtight container. Ginger root freezes beautifully when placed in a freezer bag and will last for many months.

Candied ginger cubes (above), *Z. officinale* leaves (below)

Uses

Ginger root can be used in many ways, including ground and fresh. A wide variety of ethnic cuisines use ginger root frequently as a trademark flavour. Ginger can be used in baked goods including spicy cookies like gingerbread. Japanese, Thai and Chinese cooking often requires a slice of ginger to enhance the fresh flavours of vegetables and meats. Sliced and grated ginger is a pungent addition to stir-fries, chutneys and confectionary. Ginger can also be candied for a sweet treat.

Essential oil of ginger is used in fragrances and can be used in handmade soaps, lotions or to scent spent potpourri. The oil can also be added to massage oils to ease rheumatic pain and aching joints.

Ginger root has antiseptic properties, as well as properties helpful in settling an upset stomach, indigestion, menstrual pain and motion sickness.

Heliotrope

Heliotropium

Heliotrope was introduced into cultivation in Europe in 1757, and by the 19th century, it was used extensively in gardens all over the world. It was nicknamed the "cherry pie plant" because the fragrance produced by the rich purple flowers is reminiscent of freshly baked cherry pie. That fragrance is often used as a note in perfumes even today. The scent has also been compared to vanilla, almond and baby powder. Even for the scent-challenged, heliotrope is a must-have plant and a striking contrast to many flowers, especially those with warmer colours. The end result is one colour playing off another, bringing all of heliotrope's best attributes forward.

Features

Other names: cherry pie plant
Parts used: flowers
Hardiness: evergreen subshrub grown as an annual

Growing

Heliotrope grows best in **full sun**. The soil should be **fertile, rich in organic matter, moist** and **well drained**. Although overwatering will kill heliotrope, if it dries to the point of wilting, the plant will be slow to recover.

Heliotrope is sensitive to cold weather, so plant it out after all danger of frost has passed, and cover it to protect it from frost.

Tips

Heliotrope is ideal for growing in containers or beds near windows and patios where the wonderful scent of the flowers can be enjoyed.

Heliotrope can be grown indoors as a houseplant in a sunny window. A plant may survive for years if kept outdoors all summer and indoors all winter in a cool, bright room.

Recommended

H. arborescens is a low, bushy shrub that is treated as an annual. It grows 18–24" (46–60 cm) tall, with an equal spread. Large clusters of purple, blue or white, scented flowers are produced all summer. Some new cultivars are not as strongly scented as the species. **'Alba'** is a white selection with a strong, heady scent and **'Atlantic'** produces deep purple-blue, vanilla-scented flower clusters. **'Black Beauty'** has deep, dark flowers and **'Blue Wonder'** is a compact plant that was developed for heavily scented flowers. Plants grow up to 16" (41 cm) tall with dark purple flowers. **'Dwarf**

Heliotrope grows well in containers.

Marine' ('Mini Marine') is a compact, bushy plant with fragrant, purple flowers. It grows 8–12" (20–30 cm) tall and also makes a good houseplant for a bright location. **'Fragrant Delight'** is an older cultivar with royal purple, intensely fragrant flowers. It can reach a height of 4' (1.2 m) if grown as a standard. **'Marine'** has violet blue flowers and grows about 18" (46 cm) tall.

Harvesting and Processing

The flowers can be picked throughout the blooming cycle and used fresh. They can also be dried on screens, in paper bags or in bunches hung on drying racks out of direct light.

Uses

Use the flowers in just about anything homemade that requires a scent, including soaps, lotions, hair rinses and sachets, potpourri and herbal pillows. Use dried or fresh flowers in floral arrangements with scented geraniums and any yellow-flowered stems as a colour contrast.

Hops
Humulus

Hops isn't only for the garden aficionado; it deserves appreciation for its valuable and enjoyable versatility. Hops has been used medicinally to treat insomnia, skin infections, nervous tension and anxiety. Aside from its ornamental value in the garden, hops has been one of the main ingredients for brewing beer since the 9th century, replacing bitter herbs such as *Glechoma hederacea*. The aromatic flowers have uses of their own, including in fragrances, and rejuvenating bath and hair treatments. Considering this plant's hardiness and vigour, people with any level of gardening expertise can grow hops successfully, and if you sit still long enough, you can even see it grow.

Features
Parts used: leaves, shoots, female flowers, oil
Hardiness: zones 3–8

Growing

Hops prefers **full to partial sun**. The soil should be **moist, moderately fertile**, **organically rich** and **well drained**. Divide in spring or fall, or propagate by stem cuttings in spring. If you use the cone-shaped flowers to make beer, it's easiest to begin with female starter plants because beer is made from unpollinated female flowers. If you can find only seed, sow it in early spring. It takes an average of three years for the plant to produce flowers. In regions with cold, wet winters, shield hops from moisture by growing it in large containers that can be stored in a garage or shed.

Tips

Hops is most often trained as a climber on trellises, arbours, fencing, trees, obelisks or along the side of a building. It can also crawl along the ground around shrubs and trees.

Recommended

H. lupulus vigorously produces hairy vines, densely covered in coarse, deep green, toothed leaves. Fragrant green flowers emerge in early summer; change to tan with age. This vine can reach 25–30' (7.6–9 m) heights, once established, in one season. **'Aureus'** is strictly ornamental. It bears golden yellow foliage with a mature height of 20' (6 m). If you make beer, try **'Cascade,'** or the pleasantly aromatic **'Hallertauer,'** which is used in German lagers. **'Magnum'** produces a hops that have a 'middle flavour.' **'Mount Hood'** also has a medium bitterness with a mild flavour and is best for Bavarian-style lagers. **'Nugget'** has a strong bitter

H. lupulus 'Aureus,' or golden hops

flavour that works best for stouts and ales and **'Willamette'** has a spicy aroma.

Harvesting and Processing

Pick male flowers as required and collect the female flowers in the fall. The flowers are ready when they've turned light brown, have a papery feel and are free of any dark spots. Air-dry the flowers on screens or in a slow oven (300°F, 150°C). Once dry, store the flowers in an airtight container for up to one year. The longer they're left, the more bitter they may become.

Uses

Cut and cook the young shoots that appear in spring and summer just as you would prepare asparagus. They're delicious in egg dishes and are said to purify the blood. Harvest flowers to make beer.

Cut the dried flowers and add them to arrangements and crafts, potpourri, sachets and garlands. Use the essential oil to make various bath products. To relax before sleep or relieve insomnia in general, fill a small sachet with hops flowers and tuck between your pillow and its case (a dream pillow).

Horseradish

Armoracia

Can you imagine using horseradish to brush your teeth? And you thought mouthwash was strong. Because its volatile oils block the bacterial growth that causes dental plaque, this root was once an addition to the morning repertoire hundreds of years ago. You're thankful for the makers of toothpaste now, aren't you? The medicinal value of this root has been noted throughout history, in the treatment of headaches, stuffy sinuses and bronchial infections. Today we're more accustomed to using horseradish as a condiment with our roast beef, but this herb has much more to offer.

Features
Other names: red-cole, stingnose
Parts used: roots, leaves
Hardiness: zones 3–8

Growing

Horseradish grows best in **full sun**. The soil should be **well drained, light, moist** and **of average fertility**. The root's flavour can be compromised if it's left to grow in soil that is too wet, too organically rich or too frequently fertilized. Roots left over the winter will multiply, and become invasive. Horseradish is easiest to start with a root cutting available from your local garden centre, but you can also start it from seed. Dormant roots can be planted out in early spring, spaced at least 12" (30 cm) apart.

Tips

Horseradish's broad, tall leaves and stems complement plants bearing finely dissected foliage and delicate flowers, at the back of a border. Of course, horseradish is also a fine addition to any vegetable and herb garden.

Recommended

A. rusticana is a very hardy perennial that grows 36" (90 cm) or more tall and 24–36" (60–90 cm) wide. The root can grow 24" (60 cm) deep. It produces long-stalked, tall leaves and fleshy, cream-coloured roots in small clusters. White flowers on drooping stems are produced in early to mid-summer. **'Variegata'** produces variegated or marbled leaves with creamy markings.

Harvesting and Processing

The roots can be harvested at any point throughout the growing season, but are most commonly dug up after a hard frost in fall. Fall is the best time to harvest the root because it's had the time to produce young flesh, which is less woody than an older root. Small pieces of root left in the soil will

A. rusticana 'Variegata'

resprout the following year, so if you don't want this, you may want to remove all remaining roots from the ground.

Once harvested, store the root in the refrigerator. The pungent fumes characteristic of freshly cut horseradish root are the result of oxidation.

Uses

The ground up or grated roots can be combined with vinegar, salt, sugar, dill and low fat cream cheese to create a horseradish condiment. Vinegar combined with the grated root will preserve it and subdue its pungency. Freshly grated root has the hottest flavour. Horseradish sauces are served with meats such as beef and chicken and hard-boiled eggs. Horseradish can also spice up a tomato-based sauce or be added to a sandwich to give it a little kick. Horseradish is rich in calcium, magnesium, vitamin C, contains sodium and has antibiotic qualities useful when preserving food.

The youngest, fresh leaves are mildly flavoured and tasty in salads and sandwiches.

Hyssop

Hyssopus

Much folklore is connected to this fragrant herb. Some of it is overblown or simply false, while some is correct. Its diversity has been touted since ancient times. A holy herb, hyssop was used in temple purification ceremonies. The Romans were said to have used it in their healing practices and ceremonies. Monks would plant hyssop as a border hedge in their gardens for its holy and medicinal properties. Today it is a valued herb, but for different reasons. As a companion plant, it will repel (and some people claim kill) whitefly from your cabbage plants, and, when planted close to grape vines, may increase fruit production. Even if you never use hyssop for anything but to adorn your garden, you'll still find it a sure-fire winner.

Features
Parts used: leaves, flowers
Hardiness: zones 4–9

Growing

Hyssop grows well in **fertile, well-drained** soil in **full sun**. Begin with a starter plant rather than sowing from seed, especially in zones colder than 6, so it will reach a reasonable size in regions with shorter, cooler summers. Every few years, the rootball should be dug up in early spring to cut away and remove the old woody crown.

Tips

Hyssop's beautiful pink, purple and blue flowers fill the colour void in mid-summer, perfectly complementing warm-coloured flowers and foliage in a mixed border of perennials and shrubs. This shrubby plant is also very attractive to bees and pollinating insects. Hyssop is also a great container plant for window boxes, and for locations on a hot deck or balcony.

Recommended

H. officinalis is a dwarf, semi-evergreen, woody plant that produces 24" (60 cm) tall spikes carrying narrow, mid-green leaves and topped with funnel-shaped, two-lipped dark blue-purple flower spikes. **'Albus'** produces white flowers and **subsp.** *aristatus* is a more compact selection of the species. **'Grandiflora'** produces large flowers, **'Purpurescens'** ('Rubra') has deep reddish flowers and **'Roseus'** bears medium pink flower spikes. **'Sissinghurst'** has a dwarf growth habit. **'Nectar'** is an early flowering selection and highly fragrant, **'Blue Nectar'** has bluish flowers, **'Rose Nectar'** bears pink blossoms and **'White Nectar'** has white flowers.

Hyssop oil and fragrance

Harvesting and Processing

The stem tips should be cut as new flowers open. Those stem tips should be dried, preferably in a slow oven (300° F, 150° C), or hung in bunches in a dry, shady location. Once dry, strip the flowers and leaves from the stems and store in an airtight container in a cool, dark cupboard.

Uses

Hyssop flowers are delicious and add a bit of colour to a green salad. In small amounts, the leaves aid in the digestion of fatty foods, but are quite strong. Hyssop has a bitter flavour with a hint of mint that is a great accompaniment to meat dishes, gravies, stuffings, stews and soups. It's used when making sausage, fruit pies and sugar syrup for sprinkling over fresh fruit.

Add the leaves to boiling water to create a steam bath to treat acne; the foliage has antiseptic and healing properties. A drop or two of hyssop oil in a bath is a refreshing treat for the senses.

During pregnancy, no form of hyssop should be taken internally.

Kaffir Lime

Citrus

Kaffir lime may conjure up visions of Asian cuisine. You can find kaffir lime leaves in most Asian markets and even some supermarkets, but growing this plant at home will provide you with fresh leaves year-round, whether it's outdoors in the summer or indoors in the winter. Aside from the fruit, the leaves are the most commonly used part of this plant. Kaffir lime provides the tangy, citrus flavour and scent common to many Thai soups and salads, stir-fries and curries.

If you've ever tried a dish containing this herb, you may just find yourself growing it at home to experiment.

Features
Parts used: leaves, fruit
Hardiness: tropical, zone 9

Fresh chopped leaves (left) and dried leaves (right)

Growing

As with most other citrus plants, kaffir lime prefers to grow in a location with **full to partial sun**. The potting mix should be **well drained, moist, organically rich** and **soil based**. Pruning may be necessary to keep it dense and bushy rather than thin and sparse. Keeping it smaller will also encourage it to produce more leaves.

Tips

Grow kaffir lime in a container so that you can move it outdoors long after the risk of frost has passed and back indoors long before the first frost in the fall. Plant it as a specimen and keep it in a loose, natural or topiary form.

Recommended

C. hystrix produces leathery, shiny leaves that have a teardrop shape (resembling wings or an hourglass) in mirror images. Fragrant white flowers emerge from woody stems during the longest days of summer. In the right conditions, this species can grow up to 6' (1.8 m) on dwarf rootstock, but is better kept at 4–5' (1.2–1.5 m) or

shorter to make it easier to move. It bears attractive and fragrant white blossoms and knobby-skinned, bright green fruits approximately 4" (10 cm) wide. This species also produces 1" (2.5 cm) thorns, sporadically, along the stems.

Harvesting and Processing

The leaves can be harvested all year long and used fresh, dried or frozen. To freeze, place leaves between two layers of tin foil. Dry leaves by placing them onto screens out of direct light. Once dry, store in an airtight container. The fruit rind can also be dried as you would with the leaves or the whole fruit can be frozen and taken out only to grate the rind.

Uses

Kaffir lime leaves are to Southeast Asian cuisine what bay leaves are to Mediterranean cooking. Shredded finely and added to stews and sauces, the leaves impart a subtle citrus flavour that is simultaneously assertive and delicate. For simmering in soups or curries, use whole leaves and remove them before serving. Kaffir lime rind and juice are also used to flavour curry pastes and cold drinks. The zest is widely used in Creole cooking.

Lavender

Lavandula

All parts of the lavender plant are aromatic and useful in a variety of ways. Lavender has been used medicinally for centuries to treat stomach complaints and fainting, even though herbalists were suspicious of its properties because of the essential oil's "fierce and piercing quality." Today herbalists recognize its value and use it to treat insomnia, anxiety, depression, indigestion and a variety of skin problems. Crafters have a special appreciation for lavender because of its versatility and heavenly aroma, and it has culinary uses in all things sweet. Someone was even creative enough to discover its repellent properties as a natural herbicide. Grow lavender purely for its beauty and dreamy scent.

Lavender and roses make fragrant companions

Features

Parts used: flowers, leaves
Hardiness: zones 4–9

Growing

Lavender grows best in **full sun**. The soil should be **average to fertile, alkaline** and **well drained**. In colder areas, lavender should be covered with mulch and a good layer of snow. The key to winter survival is good drainage—often, winterkill results from wet "feet," not from cold.

Tips

Lavenders are fragrant, deer-resistant edging plants. Containers filled with lavender should always be placed close to locations where you spend a lot of time, including decks, patios, balconies, windows and pathways.

Recommended

L. angustifolia (English lavender) is part of the English group of lavenders. It is an aromatic, bushy, tender perennial. It bears spikes of small flowers in varied shades of violet blue that stand above fragrant, silvery green foliage. **'Ellagance Ice'** produces white flowers with a hint of blue in a compact form (Zones 5–9). **'Hidcote'** is also compact with deep purple flowers and silvery grey leaves (Zones 4–8). **'Hidcote Pink'** has pink flowers and **'Munstead'** produces bluish purple flowers (Zones 4–9). **'Nana Alba'** is very compact with pure white flowers (Zones 5–8), and **'Royal Purple'** produces dark blue-purple flowers (Zones 5–9).

L. dentata (French lavender, fringed lavender) is a spreading sub-shrub that grows 36" (90 cm) tall and 5' (1.5 m) wide. It produces scalloped, needle-like leaves and purple-blue flowers (Zones 8–9). **'Goodwin Creek Grey'** bears silvery grey, toothed foliage and deep purple-blue flowers (Zones 7–9).

L. x intermedia is part of the lavandin group, and has a rounded form, grey-green leaves and blue-purple flowers.

Lavender blooms emerging (above), lavender topiary (below)

In the garden, lavender is a fine companion plant to thyme and to many vegetables, resulting in tastier, healthier veggies.

This hybrid will reach 12–24" (30–60 cm) heights and spreads. **'Alba'** produces white flowers and grey leaves. **'Dutch'** has dark purple flowers. **'Fred Boutin'** is a low-growing selection with silvery, woolly foliage and violet flowers. **'Grosso'** has a very strong scent with violet flowers (Zones 5–9).

L. multifida **'Spanish Eyes'** is an annual selection with green, fern-like foliage and bright blue-lavender flowers. It grows 24" (60 cm) tall and wide (Zone 9).

L. stoechas (Italian lavender, Spanish lavender) is part of the French group of lavenders. This species bears dark purple flowers and linear, green leaves. It grows 24" (60 cm) tall and wide (Zones 8–9). **'Kew Red'** bears dark magenta red flowers (Zones 7–9). **Subsp.** *pedunculata* (French long lavender) produces large magenta flowers and grows almost 36" (90cm) tall (Zones 8–9). **'Purple Ribbon'** produces large purple flowers with wing-like bracts (Zones 7–9).

Lavender-scented dream pillow (above), Lavender-scented bath salts (below)

Harvesting and Processing

Pick lavender just shortly before the last flowers on the stalks open fully, when the oil content in the blossoms is most potent. Cut the stems when it's dry and early in the day, before the heat of the sun draws out the oils. Hang bunches in a dry, airy location. Drying racks are ideal for this purpose. Once dry, either strip the flowers from the stems and store in an airtight container, or leave stems intact for arrangements. Fresh, pliable stems can be braided, twisted and knotted into lavender rope. Just ensure that the stems are cut at soil level for maximum length.

Uses

Use lavender flowers to decorate sweets or add them to the ingredients for a unique flavour. Lavender shortbread, for example, is very tasty. The scent of lavender has the power to calm frayed nerves when added to a warm bath. Lavender oil eases discomfort when massaged into rheumatic joints. Crafters use lavender and its essence in various toiletries, including soaps, lotions, bath products and fragrances. Whole stems and flowers can be braided into garlands or to fill sachets. The oil can be added to distilled water to make skin fresheners, lip balm, massage oil, antiseptic wash, foot bath and room freshener.

Lemon Balm

Melissa

This lemon-scented and flavoured herb is indispensable to those who love a touch of lemon in their food. This herb is incredibly easy to grow, regardless of what zone you live in or your level of gardening expertise. Lemony scented and flavoured herbs are usually quite versatile and can be used for cooking, and in crafts and cosmetics, not to mention medicinally. Lemon balm is even a fine companion plant to most other plants, particularly other herbs and vegetables. Things just seem to grow bigger and better and have more flavour and aroma with lemon balm growing close by. Some even say that growing lemon balm in pastures where cows graze increases their milk production. If you're without a herd of cows in your backyard, you'll still find lemon balm to be one of the most important herbs in your garden.

Lemon balm grown in a raised bed

Features
Other names: balm
Parts used: leaves
Hardiness: zones 3–7

Growing
Lemon balm prefers to grow in **full sun** but will grow quite successfully in locations with dappled shade. The soil should be **moist, fertile** and **well drained**, but it can tolerate poor, dry soils. *M.* 'All Gold' requires some shade to prevent the foliage from scorching. This cultivar may also need a little winter protection in zones colder than 4.

Taking cuttings for use will encourage dense and vigorous growth. It's best to remove the flowers as they emerge.

Tips
Lemon balm is a self-seeder and may spread throughout your garden— it's related to mint, which has a similar habit. Lemon balm doesn't possess the same invasive nature, but it may be best to prevent it from straying. Herb gardens are often the preferred location for this useful perennial, but it also works well as a fragrant filler in containers, mixed beds and borders. Lemon balm is a well-known bee plant and will attract other pollinating insects as well.

Lemon balm adds flavour to cold drinks.

Lemon balm in a mixed container with viola and pineapple mint

Recommended

M. officinalis is a bushy, dense-growing perennial with roughly textured, hairy leaves that are fragrant and flavourful when bruised or crushed. Flowers are produced but are considered to be inconspicuous. It grows 24" (60 cm) tall and wide. **'All Gold'** has yellow foliage and **'Aurea'** produces gold and green mottled leaves in a variegated form. **'Citronella'** is the most fragrant cultivar available. It has double the oil content compared to other selections and is slightly more compact in form. **'Lemonella'** is very similar to the former cultivar in aroma and overall mature size. **'Lime'** produces an aroma more reminiscent of lime than oranges, but the overall look is the same. **'Quedlingburger'** is a taller cultivar with good oil content in its foliage.

Harvesting and Processing

Lemon balm leaves can be picked throughout the growing season. Fresh leaves definitely offer the strongest flavour. It's best to harvest the leaves before the flowers emerge or open, when the essential oils in the leaves are at their most potent. At the end of the season, before a hard frost, cut the entire plant down to soil level. Spread the stems and leaves out onto a screen to dry. Once dry, strip leaves from the stems and store in an airtight container. Fresh leaves can also be stored year-round for later use by chopping them finely and storing them in ice cube trays with a little water.

Lemon balm is used to scent lotions and potpourri.

Uses

The leaves can be harvested fresh or dried for teas, both hot and cold. Custom tea blends can vary and certain flavours blend better than others. Blend one or more of the following herbs with lemon balm to find your favourite: anise seeds, peppermint, chamomile, bee balm, basil, cardamon pods, fennel seeds and rose hips. Each makes a complementary addition to the acidic, citrus flavour of lemon balm. Lemon balm leaves are also useful in flavouring desserts and savoury dishes.

Infused in boiling water, the fresh or dried leaves can be made into a rinse for oily hair, as well as a skin tonic and moisturizer; they can also be added to bath water. The dried leaves can be used in potpourri, herbal pillows and sachets.

There are may culinary uses for lemon balm, mainly in treats that require no cooking because the flavour is mostly lost when heat is added to the mix. Fresh leaves are a lemony treat when added to cool drinks, salads or crystallized for decorating desserts. The flavour is also a nice addition to citrus-flavoured marmalades and jams, fish dishes and soups. It can be combined with other strong-flavoured herbs as a seasoning for poultry, lamb and stewed fruit.

Lemon is an important and popular scent in aromatherapy. It is said to relieve depression, stress, tension and headaches, and sharpen memory.

Lemongrass

Cymbopogon

Just the thought of lemongrass makes my mouth water, reminding me of the delicious things that I love about this herb. My favourite ethnic cuisines are without a doubt Asian, but more specifically Thai, Chinese and Vietnamese, all of which use lemongrass. This is such a fresh, revitalizing and tasty plant that it is worthy of more experimentation in the garden. Crafters are also as fond of this plant. Its essence is good for the skin, giving the complexion a luminous glow, so try adding some to your bath. Medicinally, lemongrass is a tonic for the kidneys, can sooth a fever and is simply refreshing on a hot, summer day.

Features
Other names: Indian lemon grass
Parts used: leaves, tender shoots
Hardiness: annual

Growing
Lemongrass prefers to be grown in **hot** and **sunny** locations in **very well-drained, sandy, moist** soil. Water thoroughly and more frequently during dry, hot spells. Divide in spring.

Tips
This grassy looking plant is perfectly suited to warm to hot, sunny locations in your garden. Lemongrass tolerates dry areas as well. It can be integrated into your mixed flowerbeds as a foliar accent

or added to a herb garden purely for practical purposes. It can also be grown in containers, allowing you to bring it indoors during winter.

Recommended

C. citratus (West Indian lemongrass) is a stocky, clump-forming grass with hollow, cane-like stems. Long, narrow, arching leaves emerge from the base of the stems, aromatic and bluish green in colour. This species grows up to 36" (90 cm) tall or more and 12–24" (30–60 cm) wide.

Dried lemongrass and lemongrass oil

simmering soup or to hot water for a refreshing, lemony flavour. Alternatively, place bruised stems into boiling broth, soup bases and one-dish meals. To release the oils from the swollen base of the stems, bruise the outer layers with the back of a knife.

The essential oil is used to scent bath products, handmade soaps and lotions, perfumes, sachets, potpourri and room fresheners. Medicinally, lemongrass has antiseptic properties and is used externally to treat rheumatic aches and pains, and internally for indigestion and upset stomachs.

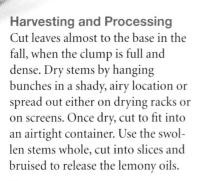

Harvesting and Processing

Cut leaves almost to the base in the fall, when the clump is full and dense. Dry stems by hanging bunches in a shady, airy location or spread out either on drying racks or on screens. Once dry, cut to fit into an airtight container. Use the swollen stems whole, cut into slices and bruised to release the lemony oils.

Uses

Lemongrass can be used wherever a lemon flavour is desired. Use the tips of the leaves, the tender shoots and whole leaves in the cooking process and discard them just before serving. Add chopped, tender leaves to steaming fish or chicken, into a

Mature lemongrass plants

Lemon Verbena

Aloysia

Lemon verbena is one of the most popular lemon-scented herbs and is also one of the most versatile. Its fresh leaves can be used to flavour oils and vinegars, drinks, desserts, stuffing and to scent sachets for year-round enjoyment. After a strenuous day in the garden or at the gym, drop a bunch of fresh lemon verbena leaves into a hot bath and the lemony fragrance will subtly perfume your skin and reinvigorate your tired muscles and spirit. The leaves have medicinal properties as well. If you're an insomniac, try lemon verbena tea as a sedative. It will also help to relieve or reduce fevers and indigestion. On a blisteringly hot summer day, it's the quintessential garnish in a cool, fruity drink.

Features
Parts used: leaves, flowers
Hardiness: half-hardy annual

Growing

Lemon verbena prefers a **sunny** location. The soil should be **light, well drained** and **moderately fertile**. Lemon verbena is best grown from starter plants rather than from seed. Wait to plant out at least one to two weeks after the last spring frost.

Tips

Grow lemon verbena in a container in colder regions, so it can be brought inside for the winter. Plant it in a herb or vegetable garden, with other herbs in a strawberry pot for interest, or by itself in a decorative container. Give it lots of room when planting it with other plants.

Recommended

A. triphylla produces pale green, narrow leaves that smell strongly of lemon. Tiny, white flowers tinged with pale purple emerge in early summer. It grows 3–4' (90 cm–1.2 m) tall and 12–36" (30–90 cm) wide.

Harvesting and Processing

The leaves are most flavourful when fresh and most intense when taken from mature plants. Pinch off the newest leaves often to encourage new, dense and bushy growth. Pick leaves before the flowers emerge or open. Flowers may not even form in a short season, but if they do, harvest them too. If you can't grow lemon verbena indoors over the winter, harvest several bunches of leafy stems, strip the leaves and chop finely. Mix them with a little water and store in ice cube trays for later use. Dry leaves and flowers by hanging bunches in a shady, airy location. Once dry, store in an airtight container.

Lemon verbena tea

Use

Use fresh leaves alone, or in combination with other herbs for tea. Add a pinch of dried leaves to stuffings, sauces, ice creams and desserts.

Crafters love this herb because it retains its strong lemony scent for years. It's a great addition to sachets and dream pillows. A potpourri of chamomile flowers, a crushed cinnamon stick, marigold petals, the dried peel of one lemon and lemon verbena leaves, with a hint of the essential oil, will invigorate and stimulate the senses. Because of its insecticidal properties, lemon balm will also ward off moths and other insects when used in sachets placed in closets, wardrobes, chests and drawers. Use the essential oil to add a refreshing lemon scent to soaps, lotions, bath products and homemade room freshener sprays.

Licorice

Glycyrrhiza

Licorice is one of those herbs, or flavours more specifically, that people either love or hate. I am one of the licorice lovers in this world. It's not uncommon to find me with a bag of salted licorice, a Scandinavian treat, or licorice all-sorts. Two of my favourite flavours of ice cream are licorice and tiger tiger, made of thick ribbons of licorice-flavoured ice cream swimming through orange ice cream. Aside from its use in tasty treats, licorice has abundant medicinal and cosmetic uses. If you're feeling adventurous, licorice may be just the thing because of its rarity in Canadian gardens and absence in our pantries.

Features
Parts used: root
Hardiness: annual

Growing

Licorice requires **full sun** but will tolerate partial sun. The soil should be **deep, moist** and **rich with organic matter**. Start the seed early indoors, so you can plant the seedlings into a container for the summer months.

Tips

Because licorice is hardy only in zone 9, it should be planted in a container so it can be brought indoors for winter. It also requires three to four years of growth before the roots can be harvested. A sunny deck, balcony or patio is the best location for this leafy herb, preferably in a south-facing position where it can receive sun all day.

Recommended

G. echinata (Russian licorice) produces pale bluish violet blossoms followed by pods covered with spines. This well-branched plant is dense and bushy, producing lush, bright green leaves. It produces violet flowers and seedpods that resemble soy bean pods. This species can grow 4–5' (1.2–1.5 m) tall and 3–4' (91 cm–1.2 m) wide.

G. glabra (licorice, sweet wood) can grow up to 4' (1.2 m) tall with a significant yellow, fibrous taproot. The sticky leaves are made up of leaflets, 9–17 per leaf. It bears short spikes of violet or white, pea-like flowers, followed by decorative brown seed pods.

G. uralensis (Chinese licorice, sweet grass, sweet herb) is the least hardy of the bunch. It grows up to 4' (1.2 m) tall and is less dense and bushy than its counterparts. Small clusters of lilac flowers are followed by interesting reddish, bristly pods.

Harvesting and Processing

Dig up the roots once the plant is three to four years old, separate the roots from the stems and dry them. Once dried, grind the roots or leave whole. Licorice can become toxic if you ingest too much of it, so make sure you research how much to take and when.

Uses

This herb will likely become one of your garden favourites. The roots are usually dried and then powdered for a variety of uses in candy, liquor and sweeteners, licorice being 50 times sweeter than sugar. Licorice extract has also been used to flavour beer and soft drinks. Crafters use licorice essence in handmade soaps, lotions and bath products.

While licorice can be used medicinally as a laxative, to balance blood sugar levels and to treat coughs and breathing problems, use it only in consultation with a qualified practitioner. Licorice should not be taken by pregnant women or anyone with high blood pressure or kidney disease.

Lovage

Levisticum

Lovage is also known as love parsley but it tastes more like celery with a peppery bite. It is native to parts of the Mediterranean, finding its way to Canada generations ago. It is one of the lesser known herbs today, but it deserves a comeback. It was once used frequently both for culinary and medicinal purposes. Lovage even has cosmetic uses. It makes a fine companion to root vegetables, having an "enlivening effect" on their flavour and overall appeal.

Features

Other names: love parsley, sea parsley
Parts used: leaves, roots, stems, seeds
Hardiness: zones 3–9

Growing

Lovage prefers **full sun to partial shade**. The soil should be **deep, rich** and **moist**. It is easiest to start with young plants, but sowing seed is an alternative. Be sure to start the seed early in spring after last frost. Divide established plants in spring.

Tips

Lovage is the perfect addition to the herb or kitchen garden. It is attractive enough to grow together with flowering perennials in a mixed border as well. Lovage can be grown in decorative containers, but keep it well clipped so it doesn't overwhelm the pot.

Recommended

S. officinale produces pale green, ornate leaflets in groups of three. It can grow quite tall in a short season, bearing upright stalks clothed in foliage. Large, flat heads of small flowers form clusters high above the foliage in summer in white and yellow. It grows 3–4' (91 cm–1.2 m) tall and 24–36" (60–90 cm) wide.

Harvesting and Processing

The leaves can either be used fresh or dried. Use leaves fresh throughout the season; chop the leaves, add water and add to ice cube trays for winter use. To dry the leaves, spread them onto screens or hang leafy stems on racks. Once dry, store in an airtight container. Use stems fresh; harvest roots and seeds at the end of the season and dry for later use as you would the leaves. Wait until the seeds have begun to turn brown before harvest and pick them on a dry day. The root should be dug after the second

Flowering lovage

or third season. The leaves are somewhat bitter after the plant has flowered. If this is undesirable, remove the flowers as they emerge.

Uses

Lovage has many culinary uses. It has been used commercially to flavour foods and drinks. The leaves and shoots can be cooked and eaten as vegetables, and the seeds can be added to soups, stews and baked goods. Chopped leaves are a delicious addition to soups and casseroles. Leafy stems can be blanched and eaten, but stay away from the central flower stems, which are inedible.

Medicinally, lovage was used to treat indigestion and is still prescribed by herbalists today in tea form to promote digestion and treat rheumatism. The perfume industry has also used the essence of lovage in fragrances.

Marigold

Tagetes

It's safe to say that almost everyone loves marigolds—it's hard not to. It may sound a little corny or trite, but bright sunny flowers are pretty hard to hate. Aside from their sunny disposition and their landscape value, marigolds have a lot to offer. Reminiscent of spicy tarragon, marigolds are a tasty treat; for those conscious of their health, marigolds also possess medicinal benefits. Tuck them into your containers, flowerbeds, window boxes and vegetable gardens.

Features
Parts used: flowers
Hardiness: annual

The petals can be used, sparingly, as a pleasant, citrus-like flavouring in salads, sandwiches, wines or as a garnish.

Growing
Marigolds grow best in **full sun**. The soil should be of **average fertility** and **well drained**. These plants are drought tolerant and hold up well in

Marigold salad

windy, rainy weather. Remove spent blooms to encourage more flowers and to keep plants tidy. Start seed indoors in spring or earlier, or plant seedlings once soil has warmed.

Tips
Mass planted or mixed with other plants, marigolds make a vibrant addition to beds, borders and container gardens. These plants will thrive in the hottest, driest parts of your garden.

Recommended
T. tenuifolia (*T. signata*, signet marigold, rock garden marigold) is an upright group of annuals that produces branchy stems with narrow, lance-shaped leaves, deeply toothed on the edges. Single flowers bearing yellow or orange petals are borne throughout the warm summer months. The species grows 12–16" (30–40 cm) tall and 12–18" (30–45 cm) wide. Hybrids are available, including the **Pumila Series**, a dwarf group bearing finely fringed leaves and lemony scented flowers. Gem hybrids are also dwarf in habit, bearing single flowers in shades of orange and yellow.

Other marigold species, hybrids and cultivars can be used for culinary purposes but taste bitter. They are favoured more as a garnish even though they are edible.

Harvesting and Processing
Marigold flowers should be used fresh. They tend to lose their flavour and colour when dried and they don't freeze well. Collect a few flowers just before you need to use them to preserve the rich colour and aroma. Mid-morning is the best time to harvest, before the temperature rises and after the dew evaporates. Once the flowers are open, they can be clipped from the stem. The outer petals and bitter centre should be removed, leaving you with the petals.

Uses
This species of marigold is used as a culinary or tea herb in some Latin American countries, and its petals add a piquant note to a salad. The petals can also be sprinkled on casseroles, soups and meat and fish dishes.

Mint

Mentha

Mint is a simple and effective herb on so many levels. It's incredibly easy to grow; in fact, it'll take on a life of its own, taking over your entire yard if you let it. The selections range from gingery flavoured mint to lemony mint, among others, and every single one is useful in a wide variety of dishes. The medicinal benefits are many, and crafters are well aware of the versatility of this herb. Just think of the many things you know right off the top of your head that are minty in flavour or scent. The possibilities are simply endless.

A bundle of herbs that includes mint makes a nice addition to a hot bath.

Features
Parts used: leaves
Hardiness: zones 3–8

Growing
Mint grows well in **full sun** and
partial shade. The soil should be
average to fertile, humus-rich and
moist. These plants spread vigorously
by rhizomes and may need a barrier
in the soil to restrict their spread.

Tips
Mint is a good groundcover for
damp spots. It grows well along
ditches that may only be periodically wet. It also can be used in beds
and borders, but may over-
whelm less vigorous
plants. To contain mint's

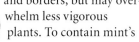

aggressive growth habit, plant it in
containers. The containers can either
be overwintered outdoors, depending
on the region, or brought indoors for
your window sill and year-round use.

For a small patch of mint in the garden,
plant it in a large plastic bucket with the
bottom cut out. Bury the bucket in the
location you desire, so the top extends
approximately 3" (7.6 cm) above ground.
The plant will be contained to the
bucket, forcing it to stay put.

The flowers attract bees, butterflies and
other pollinators to the garden.

Recommended
There are many species, hybrids and cultivars of mint. The following are only a
few of the great selections available.

M. x *gracilis* (gingermint, redmint) is a
spicy selection with a flavour reminiscent of ginger. **'Variegata'** produces
green leaves with yellow variegations.
Spearmint (*M. spicata*), peppermint
(*M.* x *piperita*) and orange mint (*M.* x
piperata citrata) are three of the most
commonly grown culinary varieties.

To control mint's vigorous growth, grow it in pots.

There are also varieties with with unusual, fruit-scented leaves and decorative varieties with variegated or curly leaves. **M. 'Berries and Cream,'** a Westerfield mint, is sweet and fruity, and **'Margarita'** produces bold, lime-scented foliage. **'Pink Candypops'** was bred with esthetics in mind, producing large, pink flower puffs in summer. **'Sweet Pear,'** another of the many Westerfield-bred mints, smells and tastes of pear.

M. suaveolens (applemint, woolly mint) produces hairy leaves suitable for candying and is considered to be superior in flavour. **'Variegata'** produces leaves touched with white and cream markings.

Blending a little chopped mint, diluted vinegar and sugar will result in a delicious mint sauce suitable for lamb dishes.

Harvesting and Processing

As with many other herbs, mint is most flavourful and aromatic when used fresh and harvested before it goes to flower. Sometimes there just isn't the opportunity to use it fresh, however. Pinch off leaves throughout the growing season for everyday use. Once the season comes to an end, or your mint patch allows you to keep pace, harvest bunches of stems to freeze and dry. For year-round fresh mint, simply chop mint leaves and add them to a little water in ice cube trays. Dried mint, if stored in an airtight container, retains its flavour and scent very well. Either hang tied bunches on drying racks or spread them out onto screens until completely dry. Strip the leaves from the stems and store in an airtight container. Wrap a few leafy stems in foil or store in an airtight bag in the freezer for immediate use; they will keep for a few weeks.

Uses

With a budding imagination, it's not difficult to find a zillion ways to use this fresh herb. A few sprigs of fresh mint added to a pitcher of iced tea gives it an added zip. Chopped leaves mixed into a stick of butter, after a brief period in the refrigerator and cut into squares, results in a tasty treat on crackers or toast. Spearmint butter is the perfect complement to lamb. Different types of mint can be mixed together to switch things up a little. Apple mint and spearmint are the perfect combination for mint sauce. Every type of mint works well with fresh fruit, tea and cool drinks like lemonade. Try new dishes with mint: sprinkle chopped leaves on new potatoes or tomatoes, egg dishes and ice cream, or mix them into cream cheese. Spearmint is a popular herb in Mediterranean and Middle Eastern cuisine. It lends a distinct flavour to meat and vegetable dishes. It's also commonly used in sauces, soups and salads. My favourite is mint tea, regardless of whether it is made with spearmint, peppermint or orange mint. Mint tea is soothing and refreshing and may relieve indigestion, promote sound sleep and, if taken regularly, ward off colds in the winter.

Mint-scented and flavoured products are abundant and for good reason. Spearmint is often used in toothpaste because it helps with bad breath, whitens teeth and conditions the gums. Mint is commonly used to scent a variety of handmade bath products, lotions and room fresheners. The leaves are a refreshing addition to potpourri and sleep pillows. A generous bunch of mint can be dropped into a hot bath as a restorative treat.

Minty ice tea (above), mint in potpourri (below)

Potted mint varieties

Nasturtium

Tropaeolum

Nasturtiums are a mainstay annual in my garden and in my kitchen. I use the flowers and leaves as garnishes, in salads and as pizza toppings. But beware of hiding insects such as earwigs and aphids—clean the flowers and leaves well. This beauty is incredibly easy to grow and will reward you with an abundance of warmly coloured flowers that are not only pretty to look at, but also pleasing to the palate.

Features

Other names: Indian cress, garden nasturtium
Parts used: flowers, leaves, seeds
Hardiness: annual

Growing

Nasturtiums prefer **full sun** but tolerate some shade. The soil should be of **average to poor fertility, light, moist** and **well drained**. Too rich a soil or too much nitrogen fertilizer will result in lots of leaves and very few flowers. Let the soil drain completely between waterings. If you start nasturtium seeds indoors, sow them in individual peat pots to avoid disturbing the roots during transplanting.

Tips

Nasturtiums are used in beds, borders, containers and hanging baskets, and on sloped banks and other poor locations. The climbing varieties are grown up trellises or over rock walls or places that need concealing.

If you find aphids on the plants, they will likely congregate near the growing tips. Cut the infested parts off and drop them in a bucket of soapy water.

Recommended

T. majus has a trailing habit. It has been greatly improved by hybridizing. The foliage of the older varieties tended to hide the flowers, but new varieties hold their flowers (available in a great selection of colours) above the foliage. There are also some new and interesting cultivars with variegated foliage and compact, attractive, mound-forming habits. **Alaska Series** plants have white-marbled foliage. **Jewel Series** plants are compact, growing 12" (30 cm) tall and wide, with double flowers in a mix of deep orange, red or gold. **'Peach Melba'** forms a 12" (30 cm) mound. The flowers are pale yellow with a bright orange-red splash at the base of each

Nasturtium seeds, fresh (top) and dried (bottom)

petal. **'Whirlybird'** is a compact, bushy plant. The single or double flowers in shades of red, pink, yellow or orange do not have spurs.

Harvesting and Processing

Pick the flowers and leaves throughout the growing season for fresh use. The seeds can either be harvested from the plant in the fall before they lose their green colour, or seed can be purchased from the garden centre. Make sure to buy seed that has NOT been treated with anything, including fungicides.

Uses

Eat the leaves and flowers fresh in sandwiches, salads or blended into dips. They should never be eaten cooked, frozen or dried. Blend them into cottage cheese for a peppery flavour or use as a garnish. Pickle the seeds and eat them as you would capers. Toss them into salads for a little bit of peppery bite.

Use nasturtium sparingly. No more than $1/2$ oz (15 g) should be consumed at one time, or 1oz (30 g) daily.

Onion

Allium

Onions are thought of as both vegetables and herbs, depending on the species, where you live and how you use them. Either way, onions are a staple in everyday cooking, offering a flavour that is unique compared to any other herb. Onions are quite possibly one of the earliest used herbs, thought to go back to prehistory, leaving us uncertain of their origins. That being said, there are quite a few onions to choose from and rightly so. Each type of onion has many uses. They're all easy to grow and require little in the way of maintenance.

Features

Parts used: swollen bulb or root, fresh juice (whole plant including leaves—Welsh onion only)
Hardiness: zones 4–9

Onions are thought to ward off colds and induce sleep as well cure indigestion. Herbalists also prescribe fresh onion juice to treat coughs, colds, bronchitis, laryngitis and gastroenteritis.

Growing

Onions grow well in locations with **full sun**. Onions prefer soil that is **well drained** and **fertile**. Seed for Welsh onions can be sown directly into the soil in spring after the risk of frost has passed. Mulch with well-rotted manure in the fall. Divide clumps every few years in spring.

Flowering *A. fistulosum* in a mixed bed of annuals and perennials

A. cepa bulb sets should be planted in their clusters approximately 12–18" (30–46 cm) apart. Don't expect too much in the first year.

Mulch with a well-rotted manure in the fall, resulting in a mass of small onions the following year. Bend over the tops of the stems in late summer to speed up the ripening process. Dry the bulbs before storing.

Tips

Onions are usually relegated to the vegetable garden but they are also a beautiful addition to the herb garden. They can also be grown in containers in sunny locations outdoors.

Recommended

A. cepa (onion) is a biennial that produces a thick stem made up of layered hollow leaves that emerge from a single bulb, 4" (10 cm) wide, at the base of the stem. **Proliferum Group**, (var. *proliferum*, tree onion, Egyptian onion) is a hardy perennial plant that can produce foliage 3–5' (91 cm–1.5 m) in height. It bears small, greenish white flowers in early summer at the tips of the leaves or stems, followed by bulbs or bulbils. Bulbs are also produced in the soil. The bulbils at the ends of the stems produce a small root system, capable of reproducing another plant if separated from the mother plant. **'Ailsa Craig'** has straw-coloured skin, a mild flavour and a rounded bulb. **'Noordhollandse Bloedrode'** ('North Holland Blood Red') also has a mild-flavoured bulb with deep red skin and pink flesh.

Onions are a staple in many cuisines.

'Sweet Sandwich' is a large cultivar with brown-skinned bulbs that become very sweet and mild after two months in storage.

A. fistulosum (Welsh onion, Japanese leek, scallion, spring onion) is an evergreen perennial or biennial that produces 24–36" (60–90 cm) tall foliage and cylindrical bulbs. In the second year of growth, it bears greenish yellow flowers in early summer. The leaves are narrow, deep green and hollow in the centre. 'White Lisbon' is a white-skinned cultivar with a milder flavour than the species and a much larger mature bulb. It grows 8–12" (20–30 cm) tall.

It was once thought that hanging a bunch of onions outside the door would ward off the plague.

Upturned carpet used as a weed barrier for onions

Onion bulb forming (above)

A selection of *A. cepa* onions

Harvesting and Processing

Welsh onions can be picked at any time throughout the growing season. The leaves are edible, too, and are best eaten fresh. Since they do not dry well, it's best to chop them finely, add a little water and fill an ice cube tray for later use. Tree onions can be picked from the stems and stored in a cool place with adequate air circulation.

Uses

Welsh onions are useful both fresh and cooked in just about any dish that requires onions, especially in Chinese cuisine. They are also tasty in stir-fries, salads, sandwiches and in any dish that uses chives.

The bulbils from tree onions can be pickled, used raw in salads for a little kick or cooked whole in casseroles, stews and soups. Just about any meat, fish or vegetable dish will benefit from the addition of this onion.

Medicinally, the Welsh onion has decongestant and antibacterial properties, similarly to garlic but a little less so. Any species from the *Allium* genus is useful to lower blood pressure and blood cholesterol. Onions are also helpful to prevent blood clotting, which can prevent circulatory diseases.

Orach

Atriplex

What is orach? Let me introduce you to this interesting and tasty plant. Orach has had a number of uses in herbal medicine over the centuries, but today it is used more for cooking than anything else. Orach can be grown as a vegetable, using the leaves as you would spinach. Because of its tender nature, you might want to grow it indoors year-round. This isn't impossible; just make sure its soil is moist and its location is bright and sunny, to prevent stretching. This way, you'll have fresh young leaves at your fingertips for cooking. When the leaves and stems become too long and tough, clip them off at soil level for use in dried or fresh flower arrangements for something a little different.

Features

Other names: French spinach
Parts used: leaves
Hardiness: annual

Growing

Orach prefers to grow in **full to partial sun**. The red-leaved cultivar benefits from partial shade. The soil should be **moist** and **well drained**. Larger leaves will be produced when grown in organically rich soil. It is best to sow seed in late spring after the risk of frost has passed. Plant seedlings or small starter plants after the last frost as well. Orach is very vigorous. Deadhead regularly and water during dry periods to prevent bolting.

Tips

Orach can be grown strictly as an ornamental or for practical use, in mixed beds and borders. Red orach in particular is stunning when mixed with yellow-leaved plants or those with flowers in fiery colours. Orach will grow quite successfully in containers. To maintain its height, pinch out the tips from time to time, which will encourage bushier growth without allowing it to outgrow its pot. Be careful not to water this plant during the hottest part of the day, as the leaves may scorch, especially the red orach.

Recommended

A. hortensis (orach) is a hardy annual that produces green, triangular leaves that resemble spades and tiny, insignificant greenish flowers. It can grow up to 5' (1.5 m) tall and 12" (30 cm) wide. **'Rubra'** is slightly smaller in overall size, producing tiny, reddish flowers and red, triangular leaves.

Use orach in salads and sandwiches.

A. patula (common orach, lamb's quarters) grows 36" (90 cm) tall and 12" (30 cm) wide, and bears spear-shaped green leaves and insignificant flowers.

Harvesting and Processing

Harvest the leaves for use throughout the growing season. This herb does not dry or freeze well. Use the leaves immediately because they will keep for only one to two days, if kept sealed in plastic in the refrigerator.

Uses

The young leaves are delicious when used fresh in salads and sandwiches. The leaves are not aromatic, but they are tasty and reminiscent of spinach, only milder. The red-leaved cultivar also lends a pleasant colour to dishes.

Medicinally, orach was said to treat sore throats and jaundice. It was also prescribed as a cure for menstrual problems.

Oregano · Marjoram

Origanum

Oregano and marjoram are two of the best known and most frequently used herbs. They are popular in stuffings, soups and stews, and no pizza is complete until it has been sprinkled with fresh or dried oregano leaves. If I had to point out a negative, it would be that the selections with the best flavour have a low tolerance to cold winters, while the hardier ones are tougher and more vigorous, but lack a lot of the flavour. What's the solution? Grow both, in fact grow all of them, because there are many to choose from, in different colours, strengths and forms.

Features

Other names: wild majoram, wild oregano
Parts used: leaves, flowers
Hardiness: zones 5–9

In Greek oros *means 'mountain' and* ganos *means 'joy and beauty,' so oregano translates as 'joy or beauty of the mountain.'*

Use these herbs to flavour oils; they can also be dried for later use.

Growing

Oregano and marjoram grow best in **full sun**. The soil should be of **poor to average fertility, neutral to alkaline** and **well drained**. The flowers attract pollinators to the garden. It's easiest to begin with starter plants, but you can also propagate with cuttings in late spring or grow them from seed. Starting seed indoors is best; plant the seedlings out when they reach at least 3" (7.6 cm) in height and the risk of frost has passed.

Marjoram is said to be a warming and relaxing herb, with antiseptic properties, useful when treating anxiety, insomnia or tension headaches.

Tips

These bushy perennials are herb garden staples. They make a lovely addition to any border or vegetable garden, and can be trimmed to form low hedges. They can also be grown in containers, making it easy to bring them in for the winter.

Recommended

O. majorana (marjoram, sweet marjoram) is upright and shrubby with light green, hairy leaves. It bears white or pink flowers in summer and can be grown as an annual where it is not hardy. It grows 24–36" (60–90 cm) tall and 12–18" (30–46 cm) wide (Zones 7–9).

O. vulgare (oregano) is a low, bushy plant that has hairy, grey-green leaves and bears white flowers. Many other interesting varieties of *O. vulgare* are available, including those with golden, variegated or curly leaves. Some of the most popular and interesting are listed here. **'Aureum'** bears golden foliage

Oregano in a mixed herb planter

O. vulgare 'Aureum' with marigold and parlsey

O. vulgare 'Aureum' trimmed into a hedge

with a mild flavour. **'Aureum Crispum'** produces rounded, crinkled leaves. **'Compactum'** has a mild flavour with a compact, dense growing habit. **Subsp.** *hirtum* (Greek oregano) is the most flavourful of all the oreganos. It has a compact habit, hairy leaves and tiny white flowers. **'Variegata'** produces white and yellow variegated leaves. **'Zorba Red'** produces dark green, fragrant leaves and reddish purple sprays of flowers with hints of white (Zones 5–9).

Harvesting and Processing

All oreganos and marjoram selections are best when used fresh. They dry well, retaining much of their flavour, but fresh is far superior. The plants should be harvested just before they are in full flower. Hang bunches of stems in a cool and airy place to dry or chop the leaves finely, add a little water and freeze them into ice-cube trays for later use. Strip the dry leaves from their stems into an airtight container for storing. The leaves can also be

Flowering oregano in a perennial bed (above), flowers close up (below)

chopped finely and added to softened butter. Refrigerate, cut into pats or squares and store in an airtight container in the refrigerator. They will last for weeks.

Uses

Oregano's pungent flavour and aroma are suitable for pasta and rice dishes, dips and just about any dish with a tomato base. It can be used in meat dishes, sauces and dressings, vegetable dishes and herbal vinegars. It's a great addition to egg dishes, salsa, chili and cheese spreads.

Marjoram has a more delicate flavour, making it suitable for pasta sauces, vegetable dishes, pizza toppings and tomato sauces where a milder flavour is desired. It's commonly used in Italian, Mediterranean and Greek cuisine and is the perfect complement to baked bread and herbal oils and vinegars.

O. vulgare 'Polyphant'

The leaves and flowers can also be added to spice up potpourri.

Parsley

Petroselinum

Though usually used as a garnish, parsley is rich in vitamins and minerals and is reputed to freshen the breath after garlic or onion-rich foods are eaten. Parsley is one of the main components of the traditional *bouquet garni*, along with rosemary, thyme, bay leaves and peppercorns. This indispensable herb is easy to grow, harvest and use in daily meals. Parsley is also a helpful companion to other plants in the garden, including roses and tomatoes, not to mention pollinating insects and bees when in flower.

Fresh parsley is an indispensable, if ubiquitous, herb in cooking.

Features
Parts used: leaves, (roots but only for
P. crispum tuberosum)
Hardiness: zones 5–8

Growing
Parsley grows well in **full sun** or
partial shade. The soil should be of
**average to rich fertility, humus-
rich, moist** and **well drained**. Direct
sow seeds because the plants resent
transplanting. If you start seeds
early, use peat pots so the seedlings can be potted or planted out
without disruption.

*Parsley leaves make a tasty and
nutritious addition to salads. Tear
freshly picked leaves and sprinkle
them over your mixed greens.*

Tips
Parsley should be started where you
mean to grow it. Containers of parsley
can be kept close to the house for easy
picking. The bright green leaves and
compact growth habit make parsley a
good edging plant for beds and
borders.

Recommended
P. crispum (curly parsley) forms a
clump of bright green, divided leaves.
This plant is biennial, but is usually
grown as an annual. **'Afro'** produces
tightly curled, dark green foliage.
'Champion Moss Curled' has finely
cut, curled leaves. **'Clivi'** is a dwarf
cultivar and **'Crispum'** is a strongly
flavoured crinkly leaved selection.
'Dark' has very dark green leaves.
'Paramount' bears tightly curled, dark
green leaves and **var. *tuberosum***
(Hamburg parsley) produces enlarged,
edible roots.

P. crispum neapolitanum (Italian
parsley, French parsley) produces flat
leaves with a stronger flavour.

Parsley fits right into a colourful container of annuals.

Harvesting and Processing

Parsley can be cut and used fresh throughout the growing season. It is most flavourful when used fresh. It can also be dried. It maintains its green colour even after drying and will keep for months. For freezing, chop fresh leaves finely, mix with a little water and fill ice cube trays with the mix for later use. This can be done throughout the season or just before hard frost in the fall, depending on how much parsley you require.

Parsley leaves can be fried and sprinkled over fish dishes for a little extra flavour and crunch.

P. crispum

Uses

Parsley has spent far too much time on the edge of a plate. Its earthy, fresh and crisp flavour is the perfect complement to so many dishes. Its mild flavour is also a great accompaniment to other herb mixtures. It works well with chervil, chives and tarragon, just to name a few. Fresh or dried, parsley was made for egg dishes including omelettes, sauces, mashed potatoes, salads, soups, pasta and vegetable dishes, especially those with poultry and fish. A tea can be made from steeping the leaves in boiling water.

Italian parsley is frequently used in Mediterranean and Middle Eastern cuisine because of its stronger flavour. Parsley is the main ingredient in a healthy and nutritious salad called tabbouleh, which also includes fresh mint. Parsley is also used quite frequently with coriander.

All parts of the plant are useful and beneficial for culinary and medicinal purposes. The roots can be boiled and eaten as a vegetable, particularly Hamburg parsley. The stems of Italian parsley can be finely chopped and used just as the leaves are used. The foliage from all parsley selections is rich in vitamin A, B and C.

Parsley has even been included in lotions for the scalp and hair before applying shampoo. This makes the hair very shiny and manageable. It is also used in herbal lotions to close large pores and as a freshener to reduce the puffiness around the eyes.

Parsley can be used in lotions to treat the skin and hair.

P. crispum neapolitanum

Peppers
Capsicum

Peppers are fruits that can also be considered vegetables or herbs. For our purposes, the smaller, hotter peppers will be our focus because they are used more often to flavour foods, whereas bell peppers are sometimes the main component of a meal. The list of uses for peppers grows every day, both culinary and medicinal. Certain cuisines— Mexican, Caribean, African, Southeast Asian and Chinese— are synonymous with peppers and their spicy heat. Aside from heat, peppers can also add earthy, spicy and sweet notes to just about any dish.

Remove chili pepper seeds to reduce their heat.

Features

Other names: cayenne pepper, hot pepper, chili pepper, paprika

Parts used: fruit

Hardiness: annual

Growing

Peppers prefer **bright light in direct sunlight**. The soil should be **moist**, **well drained** and **fertile**. Mist the foliage often when growing it indoors in regions with low humidity. Hot, dry air is detrimental to peppers. Watch for signs of shrivelled and dropping foliage and fruit. Misting will also prevent the onset of a spider mite infestation. Pinch the tips of young plants to encourage branching. Wait to plant out seedlings until the risk of frost has passed and the soil has had time to warm. To ensure good pollination, grow at least two to three plants together, either in the same garden plot or in the same window. The hotter the weather, the hotter the pepper.

Tips

Peppers are considered short-term plants; however, they can be kept for up to two to three years indoors when the right conditions exist. Place them outdoors in the summer to ensure pollination when in flower. They can also be grown in a vegetable or herb garden during the summer months. The growing season is long enough to ensure time for pollination and fruiting.

The juice from the fruit is a powerful irritant. Keep out of reach of both children and pets.

Recommended

Capsicum annuum* var. *annuum produces 4" (10 cm) long, oval leaves on thin stems in a bushy, dense form. Small, inconspicuous white flowers are followed by colourful, cone-shaped or rounded, upright fruit in shades of yellow, red and orange. There are selections available with speckled or mottled fruit as well. The following are only a few of the selections available. There are five main groups of pepper

C. 'Habenero' peppers

Young green bell pepper plant

Cayenne pepper plant in a mixed planter

cultivars: *Cerasiforme* (cherry), *Conioides* (cone), *Fasciculatum* (red cone), *Grossum* (pimento, sweet or bell pepper) and *Longum* (cayenne, chili).

'**Anaheim**' produces 6" (15 cm) long red peppers; '**Ancho**' bears brick red to black-purple fruits, 4" (10 cm) long and 3" (7.6 cm) wide; '**De Arbol**' is a hot, cayenne type of pepper, 2–3" (5–7.6 cm) in length; '**Jalapeno**' is one of the most well-known peppers, medium in heat and 2–3" (5–7.6 cm) in length; '**Jamaican Yellow**' is very hot, green to bright yellow and mushroom shaped; '**Long Slim**,' '**Mulato**,' '**Pasilla**' (poblano chile pepper) dry to a dark raisin brown, are 5–6" (13–15 cm) long and are of mild to medium intensity; '**Scotch Bonnet**' is famous for its extreme heat, and has an apple-cherry flavour; '**Serrano**' is 1" (2.5 cm) long and of medium hotness, and should be used when green or ripened to scarlet; '**Tabasco**,' the pepper used to make the sauce, produces fruits that point up to the sky, start out green, then turn yellow before ripening to a bright red; '**Thai**' is another hot selection, bearing finger-sized fruit.

C. chinense habenero produces small 2" (5 cm) long fruits. They are the hottest of the hot, up to 50 times hotter than a Jalapeno pepper. When ripe, they resemble tiny bell peppers in bright yellow.

Harvesting and Processing
Peppers can be harvested at varied stages of growth, depending on the variety and how hot you want them to be. Peppers can be used while they're still green, but wait until

Dried peppers not only spice up your food, they supply vitamins and minerals.

they've turned red if your intention is to dry the fruits for later use. Hot peppers or smaller peppers are great for drying because of their thin skin. Once harvested, the fruits can be threaded onto strings for hanging in a cool and airy location to dry. Once they're dry, they can be stored whole in a glass jar or airtight container. They can also be ground down into a powder or into flakes.

Uses

Peppers are useful in so many recipes, including meat dishes, stir-fries, appetizers, salads and sandwiches. Even the smallest peppers can be stuffed with savory mixtures of herbs and cheeses. Peppers can also be pickled and stuffed later on or just left alone as a snack.

Peppers are rich in vitamins A and C as well as in mineral salts. They also have antibacterial properties. The pungent peppers are said to

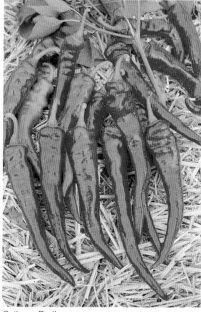

C. 'Long Red' peppers

increase blood flow, stimulate the appetite, aid digestion and fight colds, fevers and sore throats.

Perilla

Perilla

Perilla, or shiso, has been used for centuries as a medicinal plant in Chinese medicine and as an Asian culinary herb. With Asian cuisine as trendy as it is, not surprising considering its simplicity, flavour and health benefits, you'll find yourself seeing perilla in the herb section of your local market and as part of a wonderful creation on the menu at your favourite restaurant. It's also experienced a resurgence as an ornamental. Breeders have introduced more decorative selections into the market, making perilla a highly sought after annual for gardeners. Whether you plant perilla for its ornamental value in the garden or for its use in the kitchen, this useful herb will become a regular addition to your garden landscape.

Perilla in a salad

Features
Other names: shiso, shisho, green shiso, red shiso, Japanese basil, aoshiso
Parts used: leaves, flowers, seeds
Hardiness: annual

Growing
Perilla prefers **full sun or partial shade**. The soil should be **fertile, moist** but **well drained**. Soil amended with compost or well-composted manure is of added benefit. Perilla is drought and shade tolerant. It should be pinched back regularly to maintain a bushy and dense habit. Perilla may self-sow in the right conditions.

Tips
Perilla is the perfect alternative to coleus and is an ideal complement to both brightly coloured annuals and perennials in decorative containers and mixed beds. Perilla is also said to be a good companion plant to tomatoes, repelling "bad" insects. Planting this annual near or beside your vegetable garden or tomato plants is not only practical but also beautifies the immediate area.

Recommended
P. frutescens (perilla, shiso) is a vigorous annual with deeply toothed, mid-green leaves with flecks of purple. The leaves have a cinnamon-lemon flavour. Tiny, white flowers are borne on spikes in summer, but this annual is grown more for it's ornate, tasty and colourful foliage. **'Atropurpurea'** (beefsteak plant) produces deeply cut, crinkled leaves, burgundy red with pink flowers. **Var. *crispa*** (green shiso) has curly-edged leaves and **var. *crispa rubra*** (purple shiso) is very similar, but the foliage is burgundy red and the flowers are pink. Most perilla selections will reach 2–4' (60 cm–1.2 m) in height and 12–24" (30–60 cm) in spread.

Perilla is well known for its tolerance to the summer heat and will easily compete with some of the most aggressive summer annuals available.

P. frutescens 'Magilla' (above), *P. frutescens* (below)

Harvesting and Processing

Perilla can be harvested and eaten at all stages of growth. If grown strictly for sprouting purposes, then the sprouts should be harvested at the juvenile stage and used fresh. If grown for the leaves, pick them during the growing season because they are most flavourful when used fresh. They are usually gathered in bunches for cooking as greens or for use as nori or seaweed in Japanese cooking. The plant can be cut back by half mid-season, not only to encourage new, dense growth to be used later on, but also to harvest the finest leaves when they're most tender. The leaves can also be dried, just as most other herbs are dried. One method is to cut the leafy stems and tie them into bunches. Hang the bunches in a warm location with adequate air circulation. Once dry, store the leaves in an airtight container. The leafy stems can also be dried on drying racks or in the microwave oven. The flowers can also be cut and used fresh, but often our season is too short for this plant to reach a flowering stage. The seeds can be shaken loose from the seedheads late in summer or early fall for planting the following year. Shake them into a paper bag and allow to dry. Once dry, store the seed in an airtight container in a cool location.

P. frutescens 'Magilla' is grown as an ornamental plant only, and should not be eaten. It can be grown in beds and containers, however, and looks stunning planted en masse.

Uses

Having perilla leaves at your finger-tips is such a blessing since they're not always easy to find at the market, even with their burgeoning popularity. The sweet, light and spicy leaves can be used whole or chopped, for garnishing, or battered and prepared as tempura. They can also be used in sushi. The seedpod stems are commonly used as a garnish when in flower. The leaves can also be pickled as they are in Japan, and served with rice. The small flower spikes are quite tasty and can be eaten fresh as an accompaniment to salads and soups. Sweet and sour dishes are the perfect platform for the seeds, as they are used for flavouring pickled plums and other sweet and sour treats.

Perilla seeds used for pickling

Perilla seeds were recently found to contain omega–3s in their oils, similar to flax seed—perfect for lowering bad cholesterol levels.

Red Valerian

Centhranthus

Don't confuse this perennial with another useful herb called valerian, or *Valeriana officinalis*. *Centhranthus ruber* or red valerian is a culinary herb that should not to be used for medicinal purposes unless under the supervision of a medical practitioner. It is also a stunning ornamental, bearing blood red flowers that will make a distinctive display in front of a plain background. The colourful flowers are not only attractive to the human eye but also to butterflies, humming-birds and pollinating insects.

Features
Other names: bouncing Bess, bouncing Betsy, bloody butcher, Jupiter's beard
Parts used: leaves, root
Hardiness: zones 4–8

Growing

Red valerian prefers a site with **full sun**. **Dry, alkaline, sandy** or **stony** soils are perfect, but average soil is equally as good. It is known to thrive in locations with poor, compacted soil, blazing heat and poor conditions overall. It may self-seed in the right conditions.

Tips

Red valerian is the quintessential perennial border plant, for its statuesque stems and form, overall size and for its bright flower clusters. It is best planted in the back of a border, in large groupings for impact. Red valerian can be grown in containers but only in those large enough to contain it. Soil-based potting mixes are best.

Recommended

C. ruber produces deep, dark reddish pink flowers held in clusters at the tops of the stems. The stems are clothed in succulent, fleshy, pale green, pointed leaves. This species grows 24–36" (60–90 cm) tall and 12–24" (30–60 cm) wide. *C. ruber albus* has white flowers.

Harvesting and Processing

The root can be dug up in late fall in the second and third year. Once out of the soil, it should be washed thoroughly. The pale fibrous roots can be removed, leaving the edible rhizome. The rhizome can be dried, cut into small pieces or slices. The young leaves can be picked throughout the growing season. The leaves should only be used fresh and are not good candidates for drying or freezing.

Dried valerian root (above), flowering *C. ruber* (below)

Uses

Eat the leaves fresh in salads, but sparingly. They can also be boiled, but only slightly, and used in the same way you'd use spinach. The roots can be used to make soup, as they commonly are in parts of France.

Consuming red valerian in large quantities over a long time can result in illness. Leave a period of days to a week between uses, and only use sparingly.

Rose

Rosa

Roses have an incredibly rich history in the culinary arts, crafting, medicine, perfume industry and in folklore. Roses even have religious significance, because the petals were and still are, used to make beads for the rosary, hence the name. For our purposes, we'll focus on their uses in the craft studio and the kitchen. The petals and hips are both edible. The petals can be highly fragrant and have a pleasing flavour. The hips are not only filled with flavor but are also bursting with vitamins, particularly vitamin C. In fact, *Rosa rugosa* contains the highest amount of vitamin C of any plant in the world. *R. rugosa* rose hips can contain up to ¼ oz of vitamin C per 3½ oz (7 g of vitamin C per 100 g) of hips. In all the various ways they can be used, roses offer beauty and practicality.

Features

Parts used: flowers and hips
Hardiness: zones 3–9

Growing

Roses require **full sun to partial shade** in order to thrive. **Well-drained, moist** soil **of average fertility** is best. The three species of roses discussed here should be pruned in the summer after they flower.

Tips

Hardy roses are ideal for unsightly embankments or slopes. Lower growing selections are great for groundcover and erosion control, and even low hedging or border plants. Roses work beautifully in mixed borders and small groups for impact. Larger selections make beautiful specimens, particularly when in bloom.

Rose water has cosmetic as well as culinary uses, particularly in Indian cuisine. It is also very tasty when added to vanilla ice cream.

Dried rose petals in potpourri

Recommended

R. eglanteria (sweet briar rose, eglantine rose) is a species with a dense growth habit. It has arching to upright branches covered in hooked thorns. Its divided, apple-scented leaves have sticky, rust-coloured hairs on the undersides and coarsely textured surfaces. Fragrant, single, pink flowers are produced in summer, surrounding bright yellow stamens, followed by oval, scarlet coloured hips. This species grows up to 8' (2.4 m) tall and wide, and is hardy to zone 4.

R. gallica var. *officinalis* (apothecary's rose, crimson damask rose, Provins Rose, red rose of Lancaster) has a neat and rounded growth habit with dark green foliage and cupped to flat, semi-double, white and-pink striped flowers surrounding bright yellow stamens. The fragrant flowers are borne in spring or early summer, followed by

R. gallica officinalis

spherical orange-red hips. It grows 3–4' (90 cm–1.2 m) tall and wide and is hardy to zone 3. **'Versicolor'** (Rose Mundi Rose) is a compact selection with pale pink flowers striped with deep reddish-pink.

R. rugosa (Rugosa rose, hedgehog rose, Japanese rose) is a vigorous species with coarsely textured, medium-green leaves. It bears cupped, single, fragrant flowers in a medium shade of pink surrounding yellow stamens. Rounded, bright red hips are produced after the flowers. This species grows 3–8' (90 cm–2.4 m) tall and wide and is hardy to zone 2. **Var.** *alba* has white flowers, **var.** *rosea* has pink flowers and **var.** *rubra* has purplish red flowers.

Harvesting and Processing

The petals can be picked throughout the blooming cycle and used fresh. Each species, variety, hybrid, cultivar and so on has a different flavour, so pick more than a few, combine and

experiment for yourself. The darkest petals are said to be the most flavourful, but only you can be the judge of that. It is best to pick the flowers and petals mid-morning after any dew has evaporated but before the day becomes too hot. Select the flowers just as they fully open but before they begin to look spent and faded. The flowers can be cut at the stem, 4–5" (10–12 cm) from the flower base. Once the stem is cut, strip away the leaves, greenery and the stem.

The petals are best used when fresh. Ensure that they have been cleaned of any insects or dirt. Remove the base or heel, which is often white or green, from each petal.

The hips should be picked when they're in full colour, ripe and plump but not soft and overripe. Only take the hip and not any part of the stem. The hips can be used fresh or dried. They should be prepared quickly after picking by slicing and removing the blossom end. They should then be cut in half and the seeds and fibre removed with a spoon. To dry the hips halves, spread them onto a screen in a shaded and well-ventilated room. Store in an airtight container once dry.

Uses

Fresh rose petals can be sprinkled into salads as a flavour-packed addition. They can also be preserved in butter, syrup, vinegar, or they can be crystallized in sugar just as you would with violets and borage flowers. Dried rose petals can be sprinkled into herbal teas for a slightly different flavor. Dried petals and whole flowers can also be used in a variety of craft projects, including potpourri, herbal bath mixtures, sachets and floral arrangements. Essential oils can also be extracted from this plant, but are best purchased as such because it is complicated to produce the oil at home. The oil can be sprinkled into any craft you want to scent more strongly, or when something rose-scented needs refreshing.

The petals from any rose can be eaten, so if you plan to eat yours, do not spray them with any chemicals. The selections listed here are hardy, disease- and pest-resistant. Not only do they not require spraying, but they should not be sprayed with any type of fungicide or pesticide because their foliage is apt to burn.

R. gallica versicolor (Rosa Mundi) (above & below)

Rosemary

Rosmarinus

Even if you've only cooked once or twice in your life, or gardened once on a whim, chances are still pretty good that you've heard of rosemary. Native to the Mediterranean, rosemary has been used for cooking and in medicines for thousands of years. One legend tells of how rosemary wouldn't grow taller than the height of Christ, or 5–6' (1.5–1.8 m). It is one of the few herbs that is bound to be in just about everyone's pantry and for good reason. Rosemary is a versatile and tasty herb, possessing many health benefits as well as cosmetic uses, and deserving of a place in your kitchen and beauty regimen.

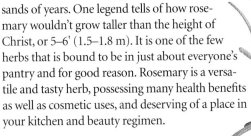

Features
Parts used: leaves
Hardiness: zone 7–9, 6 with winter protection

Rosemary-scented soap

Growing

Rosemary prefers **full sun**, but toler-ates partial shade. The soil should be of **poor to average fertility** and **well drained**. Do not let the soil sur-rounding rosemary dry out com-pletely. In zones bordering on risky, mulch heavily around the plant with dead leaves for winter protection, and water thoroughly. Rosemary can be grown from seed in early spring, but it's much quicker and easier to begin with a starter plant, depending on the zone or length of season. Cuttings can also be taken in spring to start new plants.

Tips

Rosemary is best grown in a con-tainer as a specimen or within a mixed border or bed. Low-growing, spreading plants can be included in a rock garden or can be grown in hanging baskets. Upright forms can be trained as topiary specimens. The benefit to growing rosemary in a container is controlling its environ-ment. Because it can be a little fin-icky, bring it into the house before

fall frost for winter harvest. For those lucky enough to live where rosemary is completely hardy, it can be planted into the herb or vegetable garden as a companion to sage. Rosemary is an influential plant, meaning that it will draw in honey bees for pollination and repel carrot flies outdoors and moths indoors.

Recommended

R. officinalis is a dense, bushy ever-green shrub with narrow, dark green leaves. The habit varies somewhat between cultivars from strongly upright to prostrate and spreading. Flowers are usually in shades of blue, but pink-flowered cultivars are avail-able (Zone 8). **'Arp'** is reliable to zone 7 and even 6 with adequate winter pro-tection. It bears grey-green foliage with good flavour and aroma. **'Blue Boy'** is a compact selection with a free-flower-ing habit, great for growing indoors in a container. **'Blue Rain'** is a trailing selection suitable for hanging baskets and containers of all kinds. It can reach 18–24" (46–60 cm) in width because of its trailing stems, which are loaded with

A procumbent variety of *R. officinalis* (above), *R. officinalis* 'Prostratus' (below)

light blue flowers. **'Huntington Carpet'** is a low-growing, spreading cultivar, with dense foliage and heaps of flowers. **'Majorca'** produces showy, dark blue flowers with an upright to a trailing habit. **'Rex'** is a stately selection with dark green leaves, vigorous growth habit and deep blue flowers; this one is a favourite in the kitchen. **'Santa Barbara'** is a vigorous plant with a spreading habit, and flowers earlier than most. **'Tuscan Blue'** is an upright, columnar selection with thick stems, succulent leaves and blue flowers. Its flavour and aroma are milder compared to others, but its ornamental value makes up for that. Cultivars are available that can survive in zone 6 in a sheltered location with winter protection. Plants rarely reach their mature size when grown in containers.

Harvesting and Processing

The leaves and flowers from this woody plant can be harvested throughout the growing season or year-round when possible. Strip the fresh leaves from the stems and use as they are, or dry whole stems in paper bags and store in an airtight container. Preserve fresh leaves by chopping and freezing them in an ice cube tray with a little water, or by storing a few sprigs in foil in the freezer. The flavour and aroma of the foliage is best before the plant

flowers. Individual stems or sprigs can be cut and dried throughout the summer months; harvest all of the stems before hard frost, and dry or freeze in bulk for year-round use. Collect and store the flowers as you would the leaves. If growing rosemary indoors over the winter, use it sparingly because it's receiving less light and producing fewer leaves.

Uses

The needle-like leaves of rosemary are used to flavour chicken, pork, lamb, rice, tomato and egg dishes. Chop and sprinkle the leaves over salads and lay fresh, leafy stems on cuts of meat while cooking. Add fresh leaves to herb butters, sugars and oils, cool summer drinks, marinades for fish and poultry and sauces for vegetables. The newest growth should be used for cooking while the older growth is ideal for potpourri, sachets and crafts.

Rosemary can also be used in handmade soaps, lotions, hair conditioners and shampoos and skin cleansers.

Medicinally, rosemary is said to have antiseptic and antibacterial properties. It is thought to be useful in the treatment of colds, flus, fatigue and headaches. It has also been used in a tincture to treat depression and anxiety. Infused into a massage oil, it is beneficial for rheumatic and muscular pain and great in the bath to alleviate aching joints and exhaustion.

Try adding rosemary to a martini for a flavour twist.

After a few years, rosemary will become thin and lanky. Plan on propagating or starting over about every three years or so.

Rosemary pruned into a standard

Safflower

Carthamus

Safflower is something Canadians have heard of, but often they don't know where it comes from or what benefits it has to offer. Safflower is an odd looking plant, there is no doubt. It's not one that people immediately think of when you say stunning ornamental. It is, however, a useful and tough little plant that possesses attributes useful to the crafter and artist. It's other properties are all just gravy.

Features

Other names: American saffron, false saffron
Parts used: flowers, seeds, oil
Hardiness: annual

Growing

Safflower prefers a location in **full sun**. The soil should be **light** and **well drained**. It is very tolerant to dry conditions. Seed is the best form of propagation.

Tips

Safflower is most effective when planted in large groups. Everlasting gardens are a common place to find safflower because its dried flowers are used for crafts and arrangements. It can be planted in mixed beds and borders with other annuals or perennials. Because of its sparse growth habit, it doesn't work well in container gardens.

Recommended

C. tinctorius is an erect annual that produces simple, grayish green foliage sparsely along tall stems. Atop those stems emerge thistle-like flowerheads composed of large green bracts that resemble a tightly closed flower, topped with a puff of bright yellow petals poking out of the tip. It grows 12–24" (30–60 cm) tall and 12" (30 cm) wide. **'Lasting White'** bears creamy white blossoms; **'Orange Ball'** has orange flowers and **'Summer Sun'** has bright yellow flowers.

Harvesting and Processing

Cut the flowers soon after they've opened. Hang cut flower stems to dry, either in bunches or on a drying rack. Once they are dry, gently strip the petals from the bulby bracts and store in an airtight container.

Uses

Crafters, but more specifically textile artists and weavers, love safflower for its use as a dye. Simply

steeping the petals in boiling water transfers the warm tones into the water, which can then be used to dye fabrics, yarn, thread and floss. Safflower has even been used as a food colourant. The petals can also add colour to potpourri.

Cosmetically, the dye has been used for herbal make-up and hair colour.

Medicinally, safflower is very versatile. A tea produced from steeping the petals in boiling water is said to reduce fevers. It can also act as a mild laxative. Applied externally, lotions with safflower are useful when treating bruises, skin irritations and inflammation.

Safflower petals can be used to replace saffron, and to add colour to rice and egg dishes.

Safflower oil is produced from the seeds. Used for cooking, the oil is an important part of a low cholesterol diet.

Sage
Salvia

Rosemary, sage and thyme are an everlasting trio of herbs. They work incredibly well together but are equally as tasty in their own right. Sage certainly isn't lacking in the looks department. Each species, hybrid and cultivar is unique and beautiful enough to plant strictly for its ornamental value. I usually add common or tricolour sage to my silver-and-grey-themed pots for its dense growth habit, fresh and spicy aroma and unique appeal. All sages are edible and very hardy. Talk about the perfect equation; pretty plus practical plus tasty equals a great herb.

Features
Parts used: leaves
Hardiness: zones 4–9

Growing
Sage prefers **full sun** but tolerates light shade. The soil should be of **average fertility** and **well drained**. These plants benefit from a light mulch of compost each year. They are drought tolerant once established. Sage can be started from seed in spring, but it's much quicker and easier to start with new plants.

Tips
Sage is an attractive plant for the border, adding volume to the middle of the border or as an attractive edging or feature plant near the front. Sage can also be grown in mixed planters or as a specimen, so it can be brought indoors in the winter months for year-round use.

Salvia *comes from the Latin* salvere, *"to save or to heal," hence this herb's connection to good health and long life.*

Sage butter with dried and fresh sage

Recommended
S. elegans is a soft-stemmed plant with a branching form. It bears mid-green, mildly pineapple-scented leaves and bright scarlet flower spikes. It can grow up to 6' (1.8 m) tall but rarely does. **'Scarlet Pineapple'** (pineapple sage) produces leaves strongly scented of pineapple when crushed and larger flowers than the species (Zones 8–9).

S. fruticosa (Greek sage) is a bushy, evergreen shrub with branched stems, mid-green foliage and purple, pink or white flowers. It grows up to 4' (1.2 m) and 36" (90 cm) wide (Zones 8–9).

S. lavandulifolia (narrow-leaved sage, Spanish sage) is a woody based perennial with long stems clothed in woolly leaves and blue to violet flowers. It grows up to 24" (60 cm) tall and wide (Zones 5–9).

S. officinalis (common sage) is a woody, mounding plant with soft, grey-green leaves. Spikes of light purple

S. nemorosa 'Caradonna' in bloom

Sage has been used since at least ancient Greek times as a medicinal and culinary herb and continues to be widely used for both those purposes today.

Purple sage mixed with ornamental sorrel and pepper

flowers appear in early and mid-summer. It grows 24–36" (60–90 cm) tall and wide. Many cultivars with attractive foliage are available, including the compact, golden-leaved **'Aurea,'** the silver-leaved **'Berggarten,'** the yellow-margined **'Icterina,'** the purple-leaved **'Purpurea,'** and the purple-green and cream variegated **'Tricolour,'** which has a pink flush to the new growth (Zones 4–8).

S. sclarea (clary sage) is an erect, branchy perennial or biennial with toothed or notched leaves. From spring to summer, it bears purple, pink or violet flowers with prominent lilac bracts. It grows 36" (90 cm) tall and 12" (30 cm) wide (Zones 5–9).

Harvesting and Processing

Fresh leaves are always best and should be harvested before the plant flowers, unless the flowers are being pinched off throughout the growing season. Preserve the leaves by chopping and freezing them into ice cube trays for year-round use. Dry leaves by hanging bunches loosely on drying racks away from direct sunlight and then stripping them from the stems and storing in an airtight container.

S. greggii 'Furman's Red'

Uses

Sage is perhaps best known as a flavouring for stuffing, but it has a great range of uses, in soups, stews, sausages and dumplings. Sage counteracts the richness in certain foods and aids in digestion. Combine it with other herbs, especially tarragon and marjoram, or use it on its own when cooking almost any type of meat dish.

When used medicinally, sage is used to restore energy and improve a bad memory. Drinking sage tea is commonly recommended to people who rely heavily on their memories. It's also an important ingredient in naturally based mouthwashes and gargles.

Cosmetically, it's used in cleansing lotions and deodorants, and in hair rinses to prevent the hair follicles from going grey. Sage has even been used to whiten teeth by rubbing a fresh leaf over them every day.

S. officinalis

S. officinalis 'Icterina' mixed with Italian parsley, thyme and tarrogon

Salad Burnet

Sanguisorba

This hardy self seeder adds a hint of cucumber to your favourite fresh salads. The scalloped leaves often prompt a "what is this?" response. Try adding the young leaves to tabbouleh, a Lebanese salad, and tzatziki, a Greek yogurt cucumber dip, and to garnish food that needs a hint of summer flavour. It also has the ability to freshen your breath after you have eaten you favourite garlic-laden foods.

Features

Other names: garden burnet, Italian burnet, Italian pimpernel, official burnet
Parts used: leaves
Hardiness: zones 3–8

Growing

Salad burnet is best grown in a location with **full sun** or **partial shade**. It requires **reasonably rich, well-drained** soil that is **moist** and **amended with organic matter**. It can be started from seed in spring. Cut it back as soon as the flowers begin to emerge to ensure a dense crop of foliage.

Tips

This pretty ornamental is well suited to a mixed border, herb garden, raised bed or vegetable garden. It also works well as a border plant in formal and informal settings.

Recommended

S. minor (*Poterium sanguisorba*) is a clump-forming perennial that grows 8–18" (20–46 cm) tall. It bears deeply toothed leaflets and long stems topped with clusters of rounded, deep cerise and green flowerheads.

Harvesting and Processing

Use the leaves of this plant fresh because they do not dry well. The ice cube method is the best way to preserve the fresh flavour and texture of the leaves for year-round use. Drying is possible as a last resort; dried leaves are useful mainly in cooked dishes and not for flavouring drinks or cold foods like salads. Store the dried leaves in an airtight container and discard the stems.

Salad burnet imparts a cucumber flavour to summer drinks.

Uses

The fresh leaves of this herb taste nutty with a hint of cucumber, a flavour that complements soups, casseroles, salads, herbal vinegars and cheese. The leaves are also very tasty in cabbage dishes such as coleslaw. Floating a few leaves in cold summer drinks and wine punches will add a pleasant cucumber flavour to the mix. The leaves can also be used as a garnish, and they make a great substitute for cress in sandwiches.

Medicinally, salad burnet is said to help cure rheumatism and promote perspiration when taken as a tea. Cosmetically, an infusion of salad burnet when cooled and applied to the face will help to clear the skin. Muslin bags of salad burnet in the bath will leave you refreshed and invigorated. Herbalists prescribe it to treat diarrhea and to reduce inflammation. The leaves can be applied to sores, cankers and burns.

Savory

Satureja

The savories are strong, peppery flavoured herbs. Well known for flavouring salami, they are also added to a wide variety of vegetable and meat dishes. Summer savory is considered to have the more refined flavour of the two savories, but winter savory is favoured among gardeners because it's a perennial herb. Winter savory is known to have a strong flavour that is sometimes difficult to blend into most cuisines. Summer savory is quite the opposite. Try them both!

Savory is ideal for flavouring sauces among other things.

Features

Parts used: leaves
Hardiness: zones 5–9

Growing

Savories grow best in **full sun**. The soil should be of **poor to average fertility, neutral to alkaline** and **well drained**. The flowers attract bees, butterflies and other pollinators to the garden. Start savory indoors from seed indoors approximately one month before last frost in the spring, or with seedlings once the risk of frost has passed.

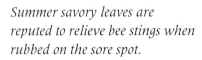

Summer savory leaves are reputed to relieve bee stings when rubbed on the sore spot.

Tips

These low-growing plants are attractive in the front of beds and borders. They don't like too much moisture in their soil, so they are better suited to a rock garden than a vegetable garden. When the soil's been prepared adequately, savory can also become an integral part of your herb garden. It will also thrive in a container, which allows you to take it indoors for the winter.

Recommended

S. hortensis (summer savory) is a bushy, aromatic annual with narrow leaves. It bears white or pink flowers in summer. The species grows up to 12" (30 cm) tall and wide. **'Aromata'** is a compact form with a higher content of oil in its leaves, resulting in more aromatic and flavourful leaves. **'Midget'** is a bushier and taller selection with a high essential oil content.

S. montana (winter savory) is a semievergreen subshrub that is treated like a perennial. It has narrow, dark green leaves that stay on the plant through early winter and are very strong and

The delicate blooms of S. hortensis (above), S. montana (below)

pungent. Pink or purple flowers are produced for most of summer. This species grows 16" (41 cm) tall and only 8–10" (20–25 cm) wide (Zones 5–9).

Harvesting and Processing

Fresh leaves can be pinched from the stems for use throughout the growing season. They can also be dried successfully in an airy place. The leafy stems should be harvested before they flower. Once dry, the leaves can be easily stripped from the stems and stored in an airtight container. Freeze leaves for later use, either by the ice cube tray method or by wrapping leafy stems in foil. The fresh flavour lasts longer when the leaves are frozen in cubes, however. The foil method will only maintain leaf flavour for a few weeks.

Young *S. hortensis* plants

Uses

Both types of savory can be used in the same way. Just be sure to taste along the way to prevent overdoing it. A little goes a long way. Finely chopped leaves, whether fresh or dried, can be added to bean and legume dishes, fish and meat dishes and into cream or white sauces. It's an ideal herb for flavouring sauces and the perfect substitute whenever pepper is required. Savory butter is very tasty and freezes well.

Medicinally, savory is said to benefit those with respiratory problems, flatulence and colic. Savory tea is useful when going through a cleanse because it's known to purify the system. The addition of savory to food will aid digestion, especially if added to bean dishes.

Cosmetically, savory has a tonic effect on the skin and can be steeped in a hot bath for this purpose. An infusion can be used to freshen breath as well.

Planting savory seeds close to other seeds or plants may inhibit their germination or growth. Savory is a good companion to onions and beans because of its insect-repellent properties.

Scented Geranium

Pelargonium

It's important not to confuse scented geraniums with the more traditional zonale or ivy leaved geraniums or perennial geraniums. They all emit a unique odour, but some are less pungent than others. For our purposes, scented geraniums are most familiar to gardeners and the public by the names mosquito plant or citronella plant, but these are just two of the many, many selections of scented geranium on the market. Unfortunately, there is no way that I could list all of the wonderful selections here, but I will list some of my favourites. Scented geraniums have much more to offer than just repelling mosquitoes, and they're incredibly easy to grow.

Features

Other names: scented pelargonium
Parts used: leaves
Hardiness: tender perennial mostly treated as an annual

Growing

Geraniums prefer **full sun** but tolerate partial shade, although they may not bloom as profusely. The soil should be **fertile** and **well drained**.

Tips

Scented geraniums blend beautifully with other annuals and perennials, both in mixed beds and containers, and they are especially effective when planted in large groups for added impact. They are always a welcome addition to herb gardens.

Recommended

P. species and **cultivars** is a large group of geraniums that have coarsely textured, fuzzy, deeply lobed or serrated, ornate leaves that emit a scent when rubbed or bruised. The scents are grouped into the categories of rose, mint, citrus, fruit, spice and pungent. In the following list, a parent of each cultivar is indicated in parentheses. Many cultivars have variegated leaves.

Scented geranium in potpourri

Pinch the plants back throughout the growing season to encourage bushier, dense growth.

Intensely scented cultivars include **'Chocolate-Mint'** (*P. quercifolium*), **'Lemon'** (*P. crispum*), **'Nutmeg'** (*P. x fragrans*), **'Old-fashioned Rose'** (*P. graveolens*), **'Peppermint'** (*P. tomentosum*), **'Prince Rupert'** (*P. crispum*), **'Rober's Lemon Rose'** (*P. graveolens*) and **'Strawberry'** (*P. x scarboroviae*).

Unique cultivars are also available. **'Attar of Roses,'** smells like roses. **'Clorinda'** has a pleasant eucalyptus scent; the species *P. grossularioides* smells like coconut. Cultivars with more subtle aromas include **'M. Ninon,'** apricot geranium, and **'Pretty Polly,'** or almond geranium. **'Pungent Peppermint'** is a strongly aromatic plant with an upright, vigorous habit.

P. 'Snowflake' (above), *P.* 'Chocolate Mint' (below)

Harvesting and Processing

Pick the leaves and use them fresh throughout the growing season. In late summer or early fall, cut the plants back by half if they are being grown in containers so they can be brought indoors during the colder months before a hard frost. Place in a brightly lit location. Cut off any stretched, weak stems, and keep plants a bit dry rather than too wet. Increase watering as the daylight increases in spring. In milder zones, leave the containers outside to over-winter, or place in a garage or shelter and keep lightly moistened. Check with your local garden centre on the hardiness of the selections you choose to overwinter outside. Mulching heavily is always beneficial for winter protection when geraniums are left in the ground.

Dry scented geranium leaves by hanging them in bunches on drying racks or on screens. Once dry, strip the leaves from the stems and store in an airtight container. Freeze the leaves whole in a layer or two of foil. They'll last for months and can be dropped into cold drinks or steeped for tea.

Uses

The leaves are commonly used with other aromatics in potpourri, sachets and herbal bags for the bath. Leafy stems can be integrated in herbal wreaths and fresh and dried floral arrangements.

Most scented geraniums leaves add a unique flavour to cold drinks, hot teas and desserts, but they are generally not eaten. Use the leaves to flavour ice creams, sorbets, sauces, fruit punches, herbal vinegars and gelatins as well as cakes and puddings, but remove them before baking. The flowers are edible.

The leaves can also be used to scent handmade soaps, lotions, bath products, hair products, herbal pillows and room fresheners.

Scented geraniums were commonly used in the Victorian era for flavouring food.

Geranium essential oils are great for aromatherapy burners and create a soothing and relaxing mood.

Scented geraniums can have unconventional (above) or conventional uses (below).

Soapwort

Saponaria

Soapwort is a herb with history. For those who have wondered what people used as soap before there was the soap we know today, there was soapwort. The stems and root of this plant, which contain a high concentration of saponins when extracted, work just as a commercial soap would. There are no current medicinal purposes for this plant and no culinary purposes to speak of, yet it's still a useful plant. As an added benefit, it's also beautiful in the landscape. It can be grown and overwintered in decorative containers and blends beautifully with bolder-leaved plants, including pulmonaria and hostas.

S. officinalis 'Rosea Plena'

Features

Other names: bouncing Bet
Parts used: leafy stems, rhizomes or roots
Hardiness: zones 2–8

Growing

Soapwort prefers to grow in **full sun** or **partial shade. Neutral to alkaline** soil that is **well drained** and **moist** is best. Start soapwort with starter plants or by sowing seed in early spring once the risk of frost has passed and the soil has warmed. Propagate by softwood cuttings and division. It can become invasive. Do not plant soapwort close to ponds because of its potential to poison fish.

Tips

Soapwort is a worthy border perennial when mixed with other perennials and annuals, as well as ornamental shrubs. It can also be integrated into the herb garden based on its useful properties.

Recommended

S. officinalis is a rhizomatous perennial with narrow, oval leaves up to 4" (10 cm) long on tall stems. It bears pale pink flowers in clusters from mid-summer to fall. It grows 12–36" (30–90 cm) tall and 24" (60 cm) wide. **'Dazzler'** produces leaves splashed with creamy splotches. **'Rubra Plena'** has double, deep pink flowers.

Harvesting and Processing

Harvest the leafy stems throughout the growing season. Harvest the rhizomes (roots) in late fall. Both the leafy stems and roots can be dried for later use.

Uses

Just as it was used prior to the production of soap in the 1800s, soapwort is still used today in the Middle East and by museums for cleaning tapestries, wooden furniture and pictures. Soapwort can be used for washing delicate items and as a shampoo, but be careful not to get it into your eyes. Crush 1/2 oz (15 g) of dried soapwort root or chop two large handfuls of whole, fresh stems and mix with 1½ pints (0.75 L) of water (if using dried stems, soak overnight first). In an enamel pan, bring the mixture to a boil, reduce heat and simmer for 20 minutes. Allow to cool and strain. It will keep for up to a week when stored in an airtight container. It can also be used as a skin rinse to relieve itchiness.

Sorrel

Rumex

Sorrel may not be one of the most well-known herbs, but it deserves wider use. It's not only a lovely, dense plant, but its tangy, zesty leaves can be used in soups, salads, omelettes and other egg dishes, or served as a side dish, similar to cooked spinach. It also holds its place in history based on its culinary and medicinal value. Written about since the 14th century, sorrel was one of the most popular herbs in France and Belgium, chiefly as a cooking herb. Recipe books from the 17th and 18th centuries include it in many recipes, and it wasn't made only into sorrel soup. If you're fond of lemony flavoured herbs, then sorrel may just be the next one to experiment with.

A facial bath made by steeping sorrel leaves in warm water

Features

Parts used: leaves
Hardiness: zones 4–8

Growing

Sorrel should be grown in **full sun**, but it tolerates partial shade. A **moist, rich, acidic** soil with great **drainage** is best.

The seeds should be sown in late spring. Remove flowerheads as they appear, as the plants can go to seed quite rapidly.

Tips

Sorrel is the perfect addition to any herb or culinary garden for its multiple uses. Sorrel can also adorn ornamental beds when mixed with various perennials, annuals and shrubs.

French sorrel is a fine companion to oregano in the garden, keeping both plants healthier and free of pests.

Recommended

R. acetosa (common sorrel) is a hardy perennial that produces large, mid-green leaves with a mild flavour. Small flowers are produced but are considered inconspicuous. This species will grow 2–4' (60 cm–1.2 m) in height and 12–24" (30–60 cm) in spread.

R. scutatus (French sorrel, buckler-leaf sorrel), the main ingredient in sorrel soup, has smaller leaves that are less bitter, with a hint of lemon. It produces shield-shaped, mid-green leaves and inconspicuous flowers. It will grow 6–18" (15–46 cm) tall and 24" (60 cm) wide. **'Silver Shield'** has silvery green leaves and only grows 6–18" (15–46 cm) in height but up to 4' (1.2 m) wide, making it a good ground cover in the right zone.

Harvesting and Processing

The fresh leaves are available for picking throughout the growing season, and are most flavourful when used fresh. Once the growing season is over, in colder zones, the leaves can be harvested and either frozen whole in foil

Sorrel can be grown in your vegetable garden (above), sorrel that has gone to seed (below)

or dried on wire racks in a cool, dark place with adequate air circulation. Once dry, store in an airtight container.

Uses

Sorrel can be eaten just as you would use and eat spinach. When used in egg dishes, the sharp flavour of the leaves is mellowed and balanced. French sorrel is still commonly used to make sorrel soup, a purèe of the leaves. A sauce made from the leaves is a delicious accompaniment to poultry and fish dishes, boiled potatoes and lamb. Young leaves can be tossed into salads and tucked into sandwiches for a bit of bite.

Do not consume sorrel in great quantities or too frequently because large doses can be poisonous. People with kidney disease, rheumatism, gout or kidney stones should not take sorrel internally.

R. acetosa (above), *R. acetosella* or sheep sorrel (centre), sorrel in a bed of mixed herbs (below)

Sorrel, like spinach, should not be cooked in aluminum cookware.

Medicinally, sorrel is said to cool fevers and aid in digestion. Cosmetically, sorrel is one of several herbs believed to retard the signs of aging because of its calcium content. It can be used in a facial steambath to help prevent the onset of wrinkles and to heal acne. It can be blended into handmade facial lotions for dry and sensitive skin or for its astringent properties. It can also be taken in tea form to help clear the skin.

In locations with excessively warm summers, sorrel leaves can become bitter as the season progresses. Mulching around the base of the plants helps to keep the soil cooler and improves the flavour of the leaves.

Stevia

Stevia

Stevia is unique among other herbs. This plant isn't used to flavour food, make crafts, scent cosmetics and bath products or fill sachets. It isn't used for anything except as a herbal sugar substitute, but this remarkable one-use plant is about to become revolutionary. Stevia contains steviol glycosides, compounds that are up to 300 times sweeter than sugar but without the calories. Now I've got your attention. Stevia powder can be bought at health food stores and used as you would use conventional sugar, but you can also grow this herb at home. It's relatively easy to grow and will help you to reduce your processed sugar intake. How can that be bad?

Features
Other names: sweet honey leaf, sweetleaf, sugarleaf
Parts used: leaves
Hardiness: tender perennial that is mostly treated as an annual

STEVIA 219

Growing

Stevia prefers **full sun to partial shade**. Since glycoside synthesis is reduced at or just before flowering, delaying flowering allows more time for glycoside accumulation. Pinching out emerging flowers will help increase leaf sweetness. The soil should be **well drained, moist** and **fertile**. Seeding stevia can be difficult because of poor germination rates. It is easier to start with a new plant, which will result in a quicker harvest.

Tips

Stevia integrates well into mixed beds and borders as edging; it has the most impact when planted in groups. Grow stevia in containers if you plan to bring it indoors for the winter. One to three plants should supply the average person with enough leaves year-round to use as a refined sugar substitute.

Recommended

S. rebaudiana can grow 24–36" (60–90 cm) tall and 12–24" (30–60 cm) wide. It produces hairy stems covered in dark green, toothed leaves. White, tubular flowers are produced midsummer. The leaves are not aromatic but are sweet to the taste. Dried leaves are even sweeter.

Harvesting and Processing

Harvest the leaves before flowering to ensure the highest concentration of glycosides. The fresh leaves can be cut and used immediately, but the sweetness increases exponentially when the leaves are dried. Spread the leaves out on screens or racks until completely dry. Once dry, they can be stored in an airtight container.

Powdered stevia leaves (above), stevia ready for harvest (below)

Uses

Powdered stevia leaves are used primarily as a sweetener in tea and coffee. Stevia does not break down when heated, so it can be used in cooking or baking without a problem. Stevia will not carmelize or crystallize, however, so some recipes will not work with stevia as a sweetener. The stems are also edible and sweet, but not nearly as sweet as the leaves.

Sweet Cicely

Myrrhis

Sweet cicely has a surprising variety of culinary uses because all parts of the plant are edible. It is also a very pretty shade plant for the garden. Historically, sweet cicely was used for medicinal purposes, but it's rarely used in this way now. The boiled root was once said to be a tonic for the elderly and teenagers. As most things change over time, so did the uses for this herb. Somehow neglected over the generations, sweet cicely lost its place in the herb and vegetable garden, but it is now making an appearance once again. Its versatility may just surprise you.

Features

Other names: garden myrrh
Parts used: leaves, flowers, seeds, roots
Hardiness: zones 3–8

Growing

Sweet cicely grows best in **partial or light shade**, but tolerates full sun in a sufficiently moist soil. The soil should be of **average fertility, damp** and **well drained**. Plants self-seed but not invasively.

Tips

This beautiful plant deserves to be included in shade gardens and borders as well as the herb garden. Sweet cicely has a long taproot, so it does not grow well in a container unless the pot is deep enough for the root to grow properly. Placed in a partly shady to shaded location, it will grow but not as vigorously as it might in the ground.

Recommended

M. odorata forms a clump of soft, fragrant, fern-like leaves. It bears airy clusters of tiny white flowers in spring. The flowers are followed by shiny, brown seeds. It grows 1–4' (30 cm–1.2 m) tall and 2–4' (60 cm–1.2 m) wide.

Harvesting and Processing

Pick young leaves at any time throughout the growing season for fresh use. Harvest the seeds when unripe or green or once ripe or dark

M. odorata in full bloom

brown. The leaves and seeds do not freeze or dry well at all, so they should both be used fresh. The seeds will last for a short time if stored in an airtight container. The roots can be dug up for drying in the fall, but only after the top of the plant has died back.

Uses

Sweet cicely leaves are an excellent sugar replacement. They can be chopped and added to salads, soups, stews or mixed into yogurt. A handful of leaves added to stewed rhubarb will reduce the need for sugar by half. The roots can be eaten raw, chopped up and mixed with salad greens, or cooked or roasted like parsnips. The slightly oily seeds are delicately spicy, reminiscent of licorice or anise, and are tasty when sprinkled onto salads. The seeds can be crushed and added to ice cream, pies and other fruity dishes.

Sweet cicely has been used for medicinal purposes. It was said to treat rheumatic complaints, stomach complaints and improve digestion.

Sweet Woodruff

Galium

Sweet woodruff is a vigorous groundcover for partially shaded, moist gardens. Charming, sweetly scented, star-shaped blossoms begin to emerge in early spring above a mat of low-growing, deep green foliage pretty enough to stand on its own. This groundcover is stunning when grown around broad leaved, foliage perennials. The decorative foliage is not only beautiful to look at, but is also a treat for the senses.

Features
Parts used: flowers and leaves
Hardiness: zones 3–8

The wiry, creeping habit of sweet woodruff makes it an excellent groundcover; it is particularly effective under trees. The white flowers seem to glow at dusk in late spring.

Growing

This plant prefers **partial shade**. Sweet woodruff will grow well in **full shade** but with greatly diminished flowering. The leaves are prone to sun scorch in strong, full sun. Soil should be **humus rich** and **evenly moist**. Divide plants in spring or fall.

Tips

Sweet woodruff is a perfect woodland groundcover. It forms a beautiful green carpet and loves the same conditions in which azaleas and rhododendrons thrive. Shear back after blooming to encourage plants to fill in with foliage and crowd out weeds.

Recommended

G. odoratum is a low, spreading groundcover. Clusters of star-shaped, white flowers are borne in late spring. Emerald green, lance-shaped leaves are borne with tiny, marginal prickles. The tiny white flowers contrast beautifully with the perky, dense foliage, creating a bright carpet suitable for any shady border.

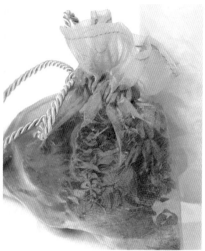

Sweet woodruff sachet (above), *G. odoratum* (below)

Harvesting and Processing

The flowers and leaves can be picked throughout the summer months and dried for later use, as the scent intensifies once dry. The leaves and flowers can be dried on screens, in paper bags or on drying racks. Once dry, store in an airtight container.

Uses

In parts of Europe, the fragrant foliage was once added to white wine in May, creating May wine. May wine is still produced today and made of Moselle, sugar and sparkling water or champagne and flavoured with sweet woodruff. The flowers also make a tasty addition to salads.

Sweet woodruff is still used medicinally today and is said to relieve stomach ailments when ingested in a tea form.

Tansy

Tanacetum

Tansies are very dependable members of the daisy family. These hard-working flowers will bloom over a long period and will stay orderly after being pinched back in May or June. Included in this flower group is feverfew, useful to many migraine sufferers, and pyrethrum, which has insecticidal attributes. Aside from their dependability, versatility and usefulness, tansies are just beautiful plants. Some gardeners aren't very keen on their aroma, but I find it irresistible.

Tansy flowers and leaves can be steeped to make a dye.

Features
Parts used: leaves, flowers
Hardiness: zones 3–9

Growing
Tansies grow best in **full sun**. Any **well-drained** soil is suitable. Very fertile soil may encourage invasive growth. Deadheading will prolong the blooming period. Divide in spring as needed to control spread and maintain plant vigor.

Tips
Use tansies in borders, rock gardens, wildflower gardens, cottage gardens and meadow gardens. Most of these species are quite civilized, but *T. vulgare* can become quite invasive. To control invasiveness, grow the less invasive cultivar or grow the species in planters and remove the flowers before the seeds ripen. A few of the species grow very tall and become a little lanky. Supporting the stems with a wire grid or peony hoop will prevent the stems from falling over.

Recommended
T. argenteum forms a low mat of finely divided silvery grey foliage. It grows 8–12" (20–30 cm) tall, spreads 12–18" (25–45 cm) and bears daisy-like white flowers (Zones 4–7).

T. coccineum (painted daisy, pyrethrum) is an erect, bushy plant, growing 18–36" (45–90 cm) tall and spreading 12–18" (30–45 cm). The main flush of white, pink, purple or red, yellow-centred flowers occurs in early summer, but some flowering will continue until fall. '**Brenda**' has red or magenta flowers. '**James Kelway**' bears scarlet red flowers (Zones 4–9).

T. parthenium (feverfew) is a bushy plant with fern-like foliage. It grows 12–36" (30–90 cm) tall, spreads 12–24" (30–60 cm) and bears clusters of small, daisy-like flowers. '**Gold Ball**' forms a compact plant bearing yellow, double flowers. '**Snowball**' bears double, white flowers (Zones 4–9).

T. vulgare (tansy, golden buttons) forms a large, erect, wide-spreading

T. vulgare

Tansy species are native to parts of Europe and Asia. They've managed to naturalize elsewhere in the world, especially in North America, to the point of becoming invasive and weedy.

mound. It grows 2–4' (60 cm–1.2 m) tall, spreads (18–36") 45–90 cm and bears clusters of bright yellow, button-like flowers from mid-summer to fall. **'Crispum'** (curly tansy) is a compact plant with crinkled, lacy foliage. It is less invasive than the species (Zones 3–8).

Harvesting and Processing

The leaves can be picked throughout the season for fresh use. Dried sprigs can be stored, whole, in an airtight container for later use.

Uses

Tansies aren't used for culinary purposes but are useful in other ways. The leaves of *T. vulgare* can be rubbed gently into the coat of your dog or cat to prevent fleas. Bunches of tansy can be hung indoors as a natural repellent to flies. Dried sprigs can be placed under carpets as a natural deodorizer. Dried and fresh leaves can be added to sachets used for repelling insects in closets and drawers. Chopped leaves and flowers can also be used to deter ants and mice in areas where they're a problem.

The roots and leaves of *T. vulgare* have been used for centuries to make dye. Both should be harvested for this purpose when fully open and most colourful, and then dried. The roots are used to make a green dye while the flowers are perfect for golden yellow dyes.

The brilliant yellow of fresh tansies (above), dried tansy insect repellant (below)

The flowers from any tansy species can be added to potpourri and aromatic sachets.

Do not take tansy internally without being under the supervision of a medical professional. An overdose can be quite harmful, or even fatal.

Tarragon

Artemisia

It's ironic that this plant gets as large as it does because you only need a tiny amount to flavour a dish. Too much tarragon can be overwhelming. That being said, there are many opportunities to use tarragon in your cooking, and you'll still have too much left over in the garden when it's all said and done. My favourite uses for tarragon are mixed into chicken salad and, in combination with fresh mint, steeped in hot water for tea. Tarragon is one of those herbs that isn't nearly as good alone as it is when blended with the right ingredients.

Tarragon is high in calcium, potassium, vitamin A, thiamine, riboflavin and niacin.

Features
Parts used: leaves
Hardiness: zones 3–7

Growing
Tarragon thrives in **full sun** but grows well in **partial sun**. The soil should be **well drained, light** and **fertile**. Tarragon has to be propagated by cuttings or division. Divide in spring. If you find seed, it's the inferior species *A. dracunculoides,* or Russian tarragon.

Tarragon is often used to flavour vinegar.

Tips
Tarragon is suitable for the back or middle of mixed perennial borders. It can also be added to herb gardens and vegetable gardens. Tarragon can also be grown successfully in containers outdoors. Growing tarragon indoors can be more than a little tricky and isn't recommended.

Recommended
A. dracunculus (tarragon, French tarragon) is the better tasting species of the two. It's important not to confuse this species with *A. dracunculoides* (Russian tarragon), which is rather bitter and difficult to dry for later use. *A. dracunculus* is a clump-forming perennial with aromatic, tender, narrow

Tarragon benefits from heavy mulching during the winter months to adequately protect the roots. Starter plants can be planted out after the risk of frost has passed.

A young *A. dracunculus* plant (above), *A. vulgare* in a pot with marigold, parsley and tarragon (below)

leaves that clothe the tall, upright stems from top to bottom. The aroma and flavour of the leaves is reminiscent of anise or licorice. Insignificant, pale yellow flowers are borne in late summer. It grows 3–4' (90 cm–1.2 m) tall and 12–24" (30–60 cm) wide.

Harvesting and Processing

As hard frosts approach in the fall and the leaves begin to wither, thoughts turn to stews, soups and meat dishes. Having a supply of fresh tarragon leaves to use all winter long will bring relief. Fresh tarragon is more flavourful than dried, but the dried leaves are good in a pinch. The leaves should be harvested throughout the growing season for immediate use. For later use, harvest the stems in late summer, stripping the leaves from the stems. Chop the

Tarragon and mint combine to make a refreshing tea.

leaves finely and mix them with water in ice cube trays for tarragon cubes. To dry, hang the stems upside down. When dry, strip the leaves from the stems into an airtight container.

Uses

Fresh tarragon can be added to butter. Combined with mint it makes a refreshing tea. Tarragon is also one of the four essential herbs in the *fines herbes* mixture, exclusive to French cuisine. The warming essence of tarragon is an ideal complement to fish and shellfish. It also works beautifully with fowl, game, egg dishes and casseroles. Fresh leaves can be added to dressings and green salads. When steeped in white vinegar, tarragon imparts a particularly savoury flavour. Combining tarragon with root vegetables such as carrots and parsnips brings out their sweetness. Tarragon is best when only briefly heated, added only in the last minutes of cooking.

Crafters have been known to use essential oils of herbs such as tarragon in herbal soaps, lotions and bath products.

The species name dracunculus, *from the Latin, means "a little dragon" and is named after this species' supposed ability to cure the bites of serpents and mad dogs.*

Thyme

Thymus

Thyme is a classic and very well-known herb that has always lent itself to culinary and horticultural uses. This versatile, hardy and tasty herb is a staple in most kitchens. All thyme species are rich in volatile oils that not only complement certain foods, but also scented products such as perfume, toiletries and potpourri. Thyme has also been employed medicinally to treat coughs, flatulence, stomach troubles, asthma and indigestion. There are a wide variety of species, hybrids and cultivars to choose from, and whether you're selecting one or more for a garden path, apothecary, recipe or craft, you'll have plenty of choice.

Features
Parts used: leaves, in some cases the whole plant or oil
Hardiness: zones 3–9

Growing

Thyme prefers **full sun**. The soil should be **neutral to alkaline** and of **poor to average fertility**. **Good drainage** is essential. It is beneficial to work leaf mould and sharp limestone gravel into the soil to improve structure and drainage.

Tips

Creeping selections of thyme are useful for sunny, dry locations at the front of borders, between or beside paving stones, in rock gardens and rock walls and in containers. Taller selections are suitable for the former but also for strawberry or herb pots, mixed herb gardens and hypertufa containers.

Once the plants have finished flowering, shear them back by about half to encourage new growth and prevent the plants from becoming too woody.

Recommended

T. x *citriodorus* (lemon-scented thyme) forms a mound of lemon-scented, dark green foliage. The flowers are pale pink. Cultivars with silver- or gold-margined leaves are available. This hybrid grows 10–12" (25–30 cm) tall and 24" (60 cm) wide. **'Archer's Gold'** is a compact plant with bright yellow, lemony foliage and pale purple flowers. **'Aureus'** produces pale, golden-green foliage and pink flowers, **'Bertram Anderson'** is a low-growing cultivar with red-tinged tips and golden foliage. **'Golden King'** is an upright cultivar with yellow-edged leaves (Zones 4–9).

T. 'Silver Posie' used as edging

T. herba-barona (caraway thyme) is a delightfully sweet selection that produces leaves that taste like caraway. It is a low-growing plant, well suited to rock gardens. **'Lemon Carpet'** and **'Lemon Scented'** produce lemony tasting leaves, and **'Nutmeg'** is also very small, producing low-growing, ground-hugging leafy stems. Its leaves taste like nutmeg (Zones 5–9).

T. **'Orange Balsam'** (orange balsam thyme) produces foliage with a potent and tasty orange flavour. It is useful for cooking, teas or for use as a garnish (Zones 5–9).

T. praecox (creeping thyme, wild thyme) is a mat-forming, creeping species with tiny, hairy-fringed leaves and purple flowers. It only grows 2" (5 cm) high but 18" (46 cm) wide (Zones 4–8).

Thyme is an attractive groundcover in perennial beds (above and opposite page).

T. pseudolanuginosus (woolly thyme) is a prostrate, woody perennial or shrublet with hairy stems and tiny, grayish green leaves covered in woolly hairs. It produces pale pink flowers in mid-summer. It grows only 1–3" (2.5–7.6 cm) tall and up to 36" (90 cm) wide (Zones 5–7).

T. serpyllum (wild thyme, creeping thyme, mother-of-thyme) is another prostrate, creeping species with tiny, hairy leaves and clusters of pink to purple flowers. It reaches ½–3" (1.25–7.6 cm) in height and up to 36" (90 cm) in spread. **Var.** *coccineus* (red-flowered thyme) produces bright crimson-pink flowers and dark green leaves that turn bronze in fall. **'Elfin'** is a taller cultivar with glossy, rounded leaves and clusters of magenta-pink flowers. **'Pink Chintz'** has grey-green, hairy leaves and salmon pink flowers (Zones 3–8).

T. vulgaris (common thyme) forms a bushy mound of dark green leaves. The flowers may be purple, pink or white. This species grows 12–18" (30–46 cm) tall and 24" (60 cm) wide. **'Erectus'** is an upright plant with camphor-scented leaves, it grows 6–9" (15–23 cm) tall. **'Silver Posie'** is the best of the silver thyme selections, bearing white variegated leaves and pale purple-pink flowers (Zones 3–8).

Harvesting and Processing

Fresh leaves can be harvested throughout the growing season by removing entire stems and stripping them of their leaves; leave them intact if you plan to remove the herb from the dish before serving, or if you're using it as a garnish. The leafy stems can also be prepared for later use by cutting the stems from the base of the plant and drying them on screens or in paper bags. Once the cuttings are dry, strip the leaves from the stems and store in

an airtight container. Fresh stems can also be frozen in a layer or two of foil and will keep for months; mix chopped leaves with water and freeze them into ice cube trays for use throughout the winter.

Uses

Thyme is a popular culinary herb used to flavour soups, stews, casseroles and roasted meat and is one of the main ingredients in a *bouquet garni*. Different types of thyme work well with different dishes. Lemony tasting thyme is often best with fish and vegetable dishes while earthy types are more suited to meat. Spicy thyme can be used in just about any dish. Throwing whole, slightly dried, leafy stems on the coals of the barbecue will flavour whatever happens to be on the grill.

Flowering thyme in a container (above), thyme in a *bouquet garni* (below)

Thyme-infused oils and vinegars are delicious on fresh green salads.

Dried thyme leaves can be added to handmade soaps, lotions, room fresheners and sachets.

Vietnamese Coriander

Polygonum

Vietnamese coriander is quite popular in Asian cooking, especially Malaysian, Vietnamese, Thai and Chinese cuisines. It's also commonly referred to as mint because of its flavour and aroma, which is a combination of coriander and mint, spicy yet sweet. If you were to travel to Vietnam, you'd find this herb in fresh salads, salad rolls and bowls of beef noodles sold piping hot by street vendors. In the Philippines, this herb is served with fertilized duck eggs (*balut*); in Malaysian cuisine, it is the essential ingredient in a spicy soup called *laksa*. Vietnamese coriander may not be as popular in Canadian cuisine, but it deserves a place in our diet. It's fresh, tasty, versatile and healthy.

Buddhist monks grow Vietnamese coriander in their private gardens for their own consumption to repress sexual urges.

Features
Other names: Vietnamese cilantro, Vietnamese mint, Cambodian mint, hot mint
Parts used: leaves
Hardiness: zones 10–11, perennial often grown as an annual

Growing

A location with **afternoon shade or filtered shade** all day long is best for this herb, but it can tolerate full to partial sun. **Moist, well-drained** soil with **average to high fertility** is preferable.

Tips

Grow Vietnamese coriander outdoors as an ornamental edging plant in mixed beds and borders because of its low-growing habit and pretty, fragrant leaves. It can be integrated into the herb or vegetable garden for more practical use. It will also thrive in containers, allowing you to bring it indoors during the colder months of the year. Bring the container in before first frost to ensure the coriander isn't damaged by the cold.

Recommended

P. odoratum is a low-growing groundcover perennial that produces distinctive, narrow, pointed leaves with unique, chestnut-coloured markings in the centre, but not every leaf bears this marking. The stems have a hint of burgundy in contrast to the bright green. It grows approximately 6–12" (15–30 cm) tall and wide. Flowers are produced but are considered insignificant.

Harvesting and Processing

Pick the leaves throughout the growing season or year-round if growing this herb indoors. Use fresh because leaves do not dry well.

Vietnamese coriander with mint and feverfew

If you cannot find a local nursery that sells Vietnamese coriander, try going to an Asian market to buy a bunch of the leafy stems. Propagate them either in water or moist potting soil until rooted. Once rooted, they can be planted in a slightly larger pots for use year-round.

Uses

This herb is slightly bitter and spicy, and is often used instead of mint, peppermint or coriander in various dishes. It is usually used fresh and added to dishes just before serving. The fresh, lettuce-like leaves are tasty in simple chicken and vegetable dishes and lend a unique flavour to sandwiches and soups. It is also said to detoxify food.

Wild Strawberry

Fragaria

Wild strawberry isn't all about the fruit, although it would be criminal to ignore the wonderful berries it produces. The leaves and roots of *F. vesca* also have medicinal benefits. There are many types of strawberries on the market, all unique in one way or the other. The selections that follow are the originals, species found in their native habitats without any alteration or interference by humans. They, too, can be cultivated in home gardens for their luxurious berries, which can be used in a myriad of delicious dishes.

Features
Other names: mountain strawberry, wood strawberry, alpine strawberry
Parts used: fruit, leaves
Hardiness: zones 4–9

Growing

Wild strawberries will grow in **full sun** and will tolerate partial sun, but with slightly less fruit production. The soil should be **humus rich, well drained** and **moist**. Sow seed indoors in late winter or outdoors in late fall. Although perennial, the plants will run their course over a few years and will need to be replaced by new plants for stellar fruit production.

Tips

Wild strawberries need a lot of room to grow, and the more plants you have, the more fruit you get. They can be successfully grown in the ground or in hanging baskets and containers. Overwinter them in a cold garage, or try growing them indoors in direct sun.

Recommended

F. vesca (wild strawberry) is a perennial plant that produces very long runners (stems that root at the nodes). It bears toothed, coarsely textured and oval leaves and five-petalled, white flowers with yellow centres. Bright red, tangy but sweet fruits are produced following the pollinated flowers. The plants themselves grow almost 12" (30 cm) tall and up to 8" (20 cm) wide but will spread via the runners to form new plants. **'Fructu Albo'** is a cultivar with unusual, creamy white fruits that taste similar to the red fruits of the species. They are said to be less attractive to birds, which may leave you with more fruit. **'Multiplex'** is an ornamental selection with double flowers and smaller red fruits. **'Ruegen'** is a very productive selection and will bear fruit in its first year. *F. v. sempiflorans*

Strawberry tea

(alpine strawberry) is a perennial that grows 2–10" (5–25 cm) tall and 6" (15 cm) wide. It bears leaves and flowers very similar to the species but does not set down runners. It can only be propagated by seed.

Harvesting and Processing

Harvest the leaves in early summer and dry them for use in tea and other infusions. To dry, place them on screens or hang on a drying rack. Pick the fruit when red and ripe, and eat it fresh or freeze it for later use.

Uses

Include dried or fresh leaves with other herbs in herbal teas; they tend to taste better in a blend rather than on their own. Eat the berries fresh or cook them into desserts, jams and preserves, juice, syrup or wine. They can also be added to summer drinks and smoothies.

Wild strawberry leaves are said to treat diarrhea and digestive problems when eaten. The leaves can also be applied to the skin to soothe blemishes and sunburn and used to whiten stained teeth.

Glossary

Acid soil: soil with a pH lower than 7.0

Alkaline soil: soil with a pH higher than 7.0

Analgesic: a pain-relieving substance

Annual: a plant that germinates, flowers, sets seeds and dies in one growing season

Apothecary: an old term for a person who prepared and dispensed drugs to the sick

Basal leaves: leaves that form from the crown, at the base of the plant

Bolting: when a plant produces flowers and seeds prematurely

Bract: a special, modified leaf located at the base of a flower or inflorescence; bracts may be small or large, green or colored

Crown: the part of the plant at or just below soil level where the shoots join the roots

Cultivar: a cultivated plant variety with one or more distinct differences from the species, e.g., in flower color or disease resistance

Deadhead: removing spent flowers to maintain a neat appearance and encourage a long blooming season

Decoction: the extract of hard or woody herb material (e.g. roots, bark, nuts, seeds) obtained by simmering the material in boiling water for about 30 minutes and straining while still hot

Direct sow: to sow seeds directly into the garden

Dormancy: a period of plant inactivity, usually during winter or unfavorable conditions

Double flower: a flower with an unusually large number of petals

Essential oil: a volatile oil, extracted by distilling a plant, that usually has the characteristic aroma of the source plant

Genus: a category of biological classification between the species and family levels; the first word in a scientific name indicates the genus

Hardy: capable of surviving unfavorable conditions, such as cold weather or frost, without protection

Humus: decomposed or decomposing organic material in the soil

Hybrid: a plant resulting from natural or human-induced cross-breeding between varieties, species or genera

Ice cube method: a way to preserve fresh herbs (mainly their flowers and leaves) by mixing them with water and freezing them into ice cubes; sometimes the herb is left whole and other times it is chopped before being frozen

Inflorescence: an arrangement of flowers on a single stem

Infusion: a liquid obtained by pouring boiling water over soft herb parts (leaves or petals) and letting them steep for 10 to 15 miuntes before straining

Invasive: able to spread aggressively from the planting site and outcompete others

Loam: a loose soil composed of clay, sand and organic matter, often highly fertile

Mordant: a substance used to fix dyes when applied to the fabric being dyed

Mulch: a material, (e.g. shredded bark, pine cones, leaves, straw), used to surround a plant to protect it from weeds, cold or heat and to promote moisture retention

Perennial: a plant that takes three or more years to complete its life cycle

Plantlet: a young or small plant

pH: a measure of acidity or alkalinity; soil pH influences availability of nutrients for plants

Rhizome: a root-like, food-storing stem that grows horizontally at or just below soil level, from which new shoots may emerge

Rosette: a low, flat cluster of leaves arranged like the petals of a rose

Salve: a soothing ointment

Seedhead: dried, inedible fruit that contains seeds

Self-seeding: reproducing by means of seeds without human assistance, so that new plants constantly replace those that die

Single flower: a flower with a single ring of typically four or five petals

Slow oven: an oven set at a temperature of 300° F or 150° C

Spathe: a leaf-like bract that encloses a flower cluster or spike

Species: the fundamental unit of biological classification; the entity from which cultivars and varieties are derived

Standard: a tree or shrub pruned to form a rounded head of branches at the top of a clearly visible stem

Strewing herbs: plants with aromatic flowers, foliage or potent oils that were used to scent clothing. or inside houses to mask odours or to repel insects during the Middle Ages; examples include basil, lemon balm, lavender and tansy

Tender: incapable of surviving the climatic conditions of a given region and requiring protection from frost or cold

Tincture: a solution extracted from plant material that has been crushed in an alcohol or alcohol-water solution

Tisane: a tea-like, medicinal drink made by pouring boiling water onto fresh or dried but unfermented plant material; sometimes also made with barley

Umbel: flowers on stalks, radiating in a U shape from a single point at the top of a stem, e.g. dill flowers

Understory plant: a plant that prefers to grow beneath the canopies of trees in a woodland setting

Variegation: foliage that has more than one color, often patched, striped or bearing leaf margins of a different color

Variety: a naturally occurring variant of a species

Index of Plant Names

Boldface type refers to the primary species accounts.

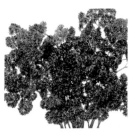

About the Author

Laura Peters is a certified Master Gardener with 30 gardening books to her credit. She has gained valuable experience in every aspect of the horticultural industry in a career that has spanned more than 20 years. She enjoys sharing her practical knowledge of organic gardening, plant varieties and gardening products with fellow gardeners.

Acknowledgements

I would like to thank my parents, Gary and Lucy Peters, for their support, encouragement and love. I would also like to acknowledge those who allowed me to photograph their gardens and plants for this publication, especially Peas on Earth Organic Garden, Greenland Garden Centre, Sunstar Nurseries and Inspired Market Gardens. Happy Gardening!

Photography Credits

AAS 61b; Jasmin Awad 84; Tamara Eder 11b, 12a, 35a&b, 75a, 115a, 191a&b, 213; Elliot Engley 26, 27a; Derek Fell 14b&c, 27b, 35c, 38, 53a, 57b, 61a, 91, 93b, 106, 121, 123, 124a, 128, 129b, 141, 149b, 165, 167c, 172b, 173b, 180a, 181b, 184a&b, 206b, 207, 221; Anne Gordon 210b; Kim Patrick O'Leary 201a; Liz Klose 8a, 24b, 60a, 117, 135,187b, 194a,195b; Debra Knapke 210a; Tim Matheson 15a,b&c, 16, 22b, 25, 30a,b,c,d&e, 33a&b, 67a&b, 72, 114, 223b; Allison Penko 83a, 115b; Photos.com cover photo, 34, 122; Elena Ray 153; Mark Turner 9606390, 206a; Robert Ritchie 190.